TWEED TRAIL CHALLENGE
River Mouth to the Source

First Instalment: The Lower Tweed Incorporating
Benchmark at Grinham's Wood

James R. A. Herriot

TWEED TRAIL CHALLENGE

River Mouth to the Source

First Instalment: The Lower Tweed Incorporating Benchmark at Grinham's Wood

James R. A. Herriot

A journey of discovery involving the Lower Tweed from the river mouth at Berwick-upon-Tweed to Cornhill and potentially onwards to the source beyond Moffat (Dumfries & Galloway). In addition to this grand expedition, there is a fascinating insight to an initiative by a small riverside community to remember and commemorate the families of past village Stalwarts who played their part during the Second World War (coinciding with the 80th anniversary of the ending of the conflict). The book's final chapter provides an insight to elements of their wartime exploits. The first instalment of Tweed Trail Challenge covers the lower reaches of the river with the author (a native of the English/Scottish Borders) providing an insightful glimpse as to what you may wish to experience and engage with when exploring this beautiful part of the world. Tweed Trail Challenge incorporates imagery of spectacular locations, buildings and wildlife encountered along the way, interspersed with anecdotes relating to such - as well as experiences appertaining to accommodation, dining and quenching one's thirst. As per an earlier publication by the author (The Sabbatical), he provides suggestions/recommendations as to books, music and fine wines to accompany those who decide to undertake this thought-provoking journey.

Tweed Trail Challenge: River Mouth to the Source by James R.A. Herriot.

First edition published in Great Britain in 2025 by Extremis Publishing Ltd., Suite 218, Castle House, 1 Baker Street, Stirling, FK8 1AL, United Kingdom.
www.extremispublishing.com

Extremis Publishing is a Private Limited Company registered in Scotland (SC509983) whose Registered Office is Suite 218, Castle House, 1 Baker Street, Stirling, FK8 1AL, United Kingdom.

Copyright © James R.A. Herriot, 2025.

James R.A. Herriot has asserted the moral right under the Copyright, Designs and Patents Act 1988 to be identified as the author of this work.

The views expressed in this work are solely those of the author, and do not necessarily reflect those of the publisher. The publisher hereby disclaims any responsibility for them.

This book is a work of non-fiction. Unless otherwise noted, the author and the publisher make no explicit guarantees as to the accuracy of the information included in this book and, in some cases, the names of people, places and organisations may have been altered to protect their privacy. All hyperlinks were believed to be live and correctly detailed at the time of publication.

This book may include references to organisations, feature films, television programmes, popular songs, musical bands, novels, reference books, and other creative works, the titles of which are trademarks and/or registered trademarks, and which are the intellectual properties of their respective copyright holders.

All rights reserved. No part of this publication may be reproduced, stored in a retrieval system, or transmitted, in any form or by any means, electronic, mechanical, photocopying, recording or otherwise, without the prior permission in writing of the publisher.

This book is sold subject to the condition that it shall not, by way of trade or otherwise, be lent, re-sold or hired out, or otherwise circulated without the publisher's prior consent in any form of binding or cover other than that in which it is published and without a similar condition including this condition being imposed on the subsequent purchaser.

A CIP catalogue record for this book is available from the British Library.

ISBN: 978-1-0682314-2-1

Typeset in Linux Libertine.

Printed and bound in Great Britain by IngramSpark, Chapter House, Pitfield, Kiln Farm, Milton Keynes, MK11 3LW, United Kingdom.

Front cover artwork is Copyright © Ollie Cowgill, all rights reserved.
Back cover artwork is Copyright © James R.A. Herriot, all rights reserved.
Cover design and book design is Copyright © David Knaggs.
Author images are Copyright © James R.A. Herriot, all rights reserved.

The photography in this book is sourced from the author's private collections unless otherwise stated.

The copyrights of third parties are reserved. All third party imagery is used under the provision of Fair Use for the purposes of commentary and criticism. While every reasonable effort has been made to contact copyright holders and secure permission for all images reproduced in this work, we offer apologies for any instances in which this was not possible and for any inadvertent omissions.

TWEED TRAIL CHALLENGE

River Mouth to the Source

First Instalment: The Lower Tweed Incorporating Benchmark at Grinham's Wood

James R. A. Herriot

Origins of the Challenge — Looking Downriver to Grinham's Wood

ORIGINS OF THE CHALLENGE

To Those Contemplating Undertaking the Challenge:

I came late in life to becoming a published author and completely by chance. During the Covid-19 Pandemic I produced an on-line journal for family and friends around the world - which was spotted by Extremis Publishing and subsequently produced in book form as 'The Sabbatical'.

Hence at the age of 70 I became a published author - and, as someone whose education came to a premature and ignominious end, my teachers would be amazed. In addition, I've not long stood down as Chairman of a company I founded with my business partner 40+ years ago, and recently completed a further book, Insights to Kitchen Design. So I found myself in need of a new project and challenge.

Tweed Trail Challenge points to my inability to sit still for long, and having the boredom threshold of a gnat. Hence my engagement with a charity 'Benchmark at Grinham's Wood,' whose aims are to promote the benefits of Paths & Benches; Woodland & Wildlife; History & Commemoration; Art & Photography; and Health & Wellbeing. A small riverside community's poignant and fitting tribute to the families of past village Stalwarts who served their country during the Second World War.

Prior to my involvement, I had no concept of 'Destination Tweed' - an initiative by 'Tweed Forum' to create a trail from the source of the Tweed to the mouth. By chance, the proposed trail could well travel through the 'Benchmark at Grinham's Wood' project - hence my decision to find out more by looking into this and subsequently recording what we (my wife Debbie & I) came across on our travels.

Our original intention related to investigating the complete trail from river mouth to the source. Also to produce imagery/photography highlighting memorable aspects. Plus compiling a list of books, classical & contemporary compositions, and wines to accompany us on our journey. Finally, the little matter of writing a book to record the stories of what we encountered along the way.

This first instalment of Tweed Trail Challenge initially relates to the Lower Tweed from Berwick-upon-Tweed to Cornhill. The reason being, at the time of compiling the book, Destination Tweed had as yet to finalise the route of their proposed Trail - but with there being an existing Lower Tweed Trail we decided to look into what this involved. Which means its possible further instalments may yet appear.

At the age of 70 I became a published author – completely by chance.

An individual's rationale to engage may differ widely, from merely reading the book to those wishing to complete our Lower Tweed journey in a single undertaking. Others may split this into various legs and return on a number of occasions. Specific towns, stately buildings or locations may prove more apt and of interest for some. Engaging with our eclectic choice of books, music, or wines in one's own home is always a further option.

The Covid-19 Pandemic and Lockdowns made Debbie and I aware of how lucky we are to live in such an amazing part of the world (The English/Scottish Borders) – and our wish to share this with others. Hence Tweed Trail Challenge being open to all and in whatever format best suits.

Enjoy.

James R.A. Herriot

DEDICATION

This book is dedicated to the 'Youth of Today and Yesterday' – and, for some (hopefully), provide an insight into the experiences of others, and may help put one's own issues and problems into perspective. Also to 'Sassy,' our guide and companion throughout our Lower Tweed Trail journey.

ACKNOWLEDGEMENTS

I would like to acknowledge 3 people without whom my 1st two books - never mind this my 3rd would not have been possible. Without the support and belief of Julie and Tom Christie from Extremis Publishing regards 'Tweed Trail Challenge' along with my previous 2 books: These would simply not have come about – I cannot thank you enough for all your input and efforts.

The 3rd person is David Knaggs my friend and colleague for all his encouragement and support along with his mastery and skill in relation to the graphics and typesetting of all 3 books. Your wizardry deserves recognition and a critical aspect as to making each one of these projects come to life. I cannot thank you enough or put into words how much I appreciate your amazing work.

With regards to 'Tweed Trail Challenge' there are 2 other people I must acknowledge who have enabled the project to reach new heights: These being Ronnie Hek (Wildlife Photographer) and Ollie Cowgill (Drone Photographer) – each of whom is a master of their craft and whose work speaks volumes. A massive thank you to you both for all your input and help.

Finally to my dear and long-suffering wife (Debbie) who joined me on the journey and has supported all my endeavours in making 'Tweed Trail Challenge' a reality. Your tutelage and understanding over half a century + has played a vital part in expanding my capabilities: Who would ever have thought (all those years ago) that an uneducated philistine - could become a published author?

The picture depicts Petty Officer Bill Cockburn (1919 to 2005), a Horncliffe Stalwart who as can be deduced from the image was very much the younger generation when he first served with the Royal Navy aboard minesweepers in WW2 - having signed-up at the tender age of nineteen. This image aptly reflects that Horncliffe's Stalwart generation were once 'The Youth of Today'.

A THOUGHT FOR THE YOUTH OF TODAY & YESTERDAY

THE WORLD IS YOUR OYSTER... DO WITH IT WHAT YOU CAN... WITH AN OPEN AND INQUIRING MIND.

(The relevance of the above statements to be revealed as the book progresses)

The Benchmark at Grinham's Wood Trustees were asked at one point to clarify and explain the reference within the introductory leaflet to their community project in relation to 'A Thought for the Youth of Today & Yesterday'. I believe it worthwhile sharing their response:

"Our statement 'A Thought for the Youth of Today & Yesterday' relates to the Stalwarts' stories and their wives, partners and families recorded alongside each memorial bench. They having once been the young generation (now deceased), also their children who at one point where the same (now the older generation), their grandchildren no longer the young generation (now approaching middle age), and finally the Stalwarts, great grandchildren being the current younger generation. The aim and intention of the Trustees being to point out all generations were once young and a rite of passage for all. Hence learning from current or prior generations can prove beneficial - no matter one's age."

Berwick Bridges by Ollie Cowgill

1 — 001 Lighthouse

TWEED TRAIL CHALLENGE 01
BERWICK-UPON-TWEED

Our epic ramble commences on the East Coast at the mouth of the river at Berwick-upon-Tweed (Northumberland), with the ultimate (at some stage) destination 113 miles west - being the source of the Tweed beyond Moffat (Dumfries & Galloway). East to west would appear the expected and natural direction of travel, but we suggest a slight deviation by first heading due east and arguably beyond the mouth of the Tweed, out into the North Sea.

For those not au-fait with Berwick-upon-Tweed, the town has a magnificent pier and lighthouse, the former completed in 1821 and the lighthouse a few years later. The pier is over half a mile long, hence the ability to go beyond the river mouth. We felt this to be the natural starting point for our venture and exploration of the Lower Tweed – and were rewarded with sighting a pod of dolphins just out to sea beyond the lighthouse.

A circuit of the lighthouse is the point of departure and beginning of our journey to learn more about the Borderlands and the many delights that abound in this special part of the world. Out of interest, attached to the Lighthouse is an interpretation panel pointing out an alternative trail with which you may wish to engage - 'The Lowry Trail,' which celebrates L.S. Lowry, the renowned British artist, and his involvement with Berwick over many years.

The Lowry Trail celebrates L.S. Lowry's 40-year love affair with Berwick — capturing the town in a series of evocative paintings.

I should point out the Lowry Trail adds approximately five miles to your overall journey, but to see Berwick at its best and learn more about this fascinating town, it will prove (we believe) a worthwhile option. The next Lowry panel can be found behind the pier, and explains the 'Lowry Shelter'. In 1999, the Town Council decided to have this demolished; a national outcry ensued, which led to its restoration by the Berwick-upon-Tweed Preservation Trust.

The re-building of the 'Lowry Shelter' and its launch led to uncovering L.S. Lowry's involvement in Berwick over a period of 40 years and the various paintings he produced of the town, subsequently leading to the creation of the 'Lowry Trail'. But enough of Lowry and his Trail – we leave you to find out more. However, we will utilise the route to identify and point out a number of other outstanding historic buildings and fortifications that abound within the town.

1 — 003 Ramparts   1 — 004 Lion House & Magazine   1 — 005 Barracks

To follow the Lowry Trail involves going uphill from the shelter, across the cricket pitch, and a little further on you will come across the Elizabethan ramparts. These are on an epic scale and the only one of their type in the United Kingdom. Queen Elizabeth I is reputed to have invested 25% of her total military budget on the creation of the fortifications. On ascending the steps, you will find the Lion House and Gunpowder Magazine with information panels explaining more.

An original Lowry painting of Berwick — unknown at the time of the Trail's creation — is on display in the Barracks.

Continue north along the walls and you come across the 'Barracks,' which demonstrate Berwick's military importance in days gone by. These now house the KOSB's (Kings Own Scottish Borderers) Regimental Museum, as well as the Berwick Museum. An original Lowry painting of Berwick (unknown at the time of the Trail's creation) is on display - alongside works by Degas, Boudin and Daubigny, the latter three donated to the town by the late Lord Burrell.

Berwick is full of interesting buildings, with a good example found immediately opposite the barracks. This is one of the few churches constructed in Cromwell's time and, following the puritanical philosophy of that era, was built without a steeple. Around the corner is the recent conversion by an enlightened and respected local builder of the civic offices, which originally housed the court and jail. If you look closely, Berwick has many fascinating architectural gems.

The Old Bridge, New Bridge & Royal Border Bridge are all truly emblematic of Berwick and its story.

1 — 008 Berwick Bridges

1 — 006 Parish Church

Back on the ramparts, you come across a spectacular view of Berwick's High Street and Town Hall – once more immortalised by Lowry. Further on is an amazing vista of the river and the three bridges, this being from Megs Mount: The Old Bridge, New Bridge and Royal Border Bridge are all truly emblematic of Berwick and its story.

1 — 007 High Street

Prior to heading down Bank Hill under the New Bridge and to the Old Bridge, look for an imposing statue on your right. The inscription states: 'Annie - Lady Jerningham of Longridge Towers, Berwick-upon-Tweed – 9th October 1902. Presented to the Town of Berwick-upon-Tweed by Sir Hubert Jerningham KC MC Late and Last Member of Parliament for the Borough'. The pair's relevance and relationship with the area will be revealed as our journey proceeds.

On descending the hill, having passed under the New Bridge, there is an interesting entrance to a building set into the bank with a set of wrought iron gates. Peer inside, and you will see a cavernous and impressive interior – this being an ice-house, a legacy and homage to Berwick's past which relates to the salmon fishing industry.

1 — 00 9 Lady Jerningham

Sallyport and Dewar's Lane — both painted by Lowry — reveal Berwick's charm in every corner.

1 — 010 Audela

1 — 011 Dewar's Lane

On reaching the Old Bridge a Lowry panel identifies the original home of Berwick Cockles (a local confectionary) and now Audela - the restaurant at which we were booked to dine later that day. Descending the walls at this point and exploring the various vennels and passageways introduces you to Sallyport and Dewar's Lane - both painted by Lowry (on more than one occasion). Pay a visit to the Dewars Lane Granary café and exhibition venue to learn more.

1 — 012 Old Bridge

1 — 013 Walls & Chandelry

1 — 014 Walls & Pier

Prior to crossing the Old Bridge (which recently celebrated its 400th anniversary) having been built in the reign of James VI of Scotland and 1st of England, we first advocate completing your circumnavigation of the Elizabethan ramparts to take in various unusual buildings and scenes - as demonstrated by the imagery. Also wander along the Quayside and pay a visit to the Quayside Lookout Café converted from a Gent's Toilet by the Berwick-upon-Tweed Preservation Trust.

At the right time of year, when crossing the river to Tweedmouth and Spittal, there is an opportunity to see a centuries old and traditional way of life: salmon fishing via coble and net, once an integral aspect of Berwick's history, employment and economic wellbeing. Gardo (Garde) is the last operational fishing station on the river Tweed.

While on the ramparts, crossing the bridge or walking the south bank of the river, look out for an unusual spectacle - Berwick's mute swan population is reputed to be the second largest in the UK. There are around 200 permanent residents, but the size of the herd increases in late summer and throughout the winter, and at peak times the number can reputably go up to 800.

The second half of the Lowry Trail is to be found on the south side of the river (which involves the hamlets of Tweedmouth & Spittal), and is worth engaging with to understand the diverse nature and history of this fascinating border town prior to departing on your Lower Tweed journey. I leave you with imagery of three vistas involving L.S. Lowry (recorded by him many years ago) to demonstrate what you will encounter:

Spittal's majestic promenade shows that Lowry's reputation for painting only gloom and despair is not strictly correct.

The first is a typical Lowry street scene and could easily be in Salford (his home town) - but actually depicts a vennel off Main Street, Tweedmouth. Further along the riverfront, on the side of the RNLI station, you come across a Lowry panel displaying a self-portrait and a photograph of the artist standing on this particular jetty. The final image involves Spittal's majestic promenade and demonstrates that Lowry's reputation of only painting gloom and despair is not strictly correct.

1 — 017 RNLI Jetty

1 — 018 Promenade

TWEED TRAIL CHALLENGE 01
BERWICK-UPON-TWEED

Authors & Books
Rambling Man – Billy Connolly

A recent purchase: A copy of the Big Yin's latest book. The title apt in relation to our exploration of the Lower Tweed. For those like me with a love of the countryside, places of interest and people, Billy's insightful words are worth investigating. I should explain I'm a fan - The Sabbatical previously featuring two books relating to his eventful life.

Musicians & Popular Music
Eurythmics – Sweet Dreams (Are Made of These)

This song takes Debbie and I back many years; Annie Lennox and Dave Stewart's music means much to us, and we can highly recommend it. The title 'Sweet Dreams' is something we hope our journey will conjure up for years to come.

Composers & Classical Music
Yann Tiersen – La Valse d'Amelie

An interesting piece of music which seems to typify and exemplify the sense of adventure and excitement we feel in relation to embarking on our new venture and learning more about both the Tweed and the Borderlands.

Fine Wine
Auxey-Duresse, Les Boutonniers, Domaine Lafouge, 2019 (France)

'Audela' is a favoured Berwick restaurant of ours, and an ideal stepping-off point in relation to seeking out other culinary delights on our exploration of the Lower Tweed. The wine is a recommendation from our son (a fine wine specialist), and proved perfect alongside our excellent food.

Kingfisher by Ronnie Hek

2 — 001 Royal Border Bridge

TWEED TRAIL CHALLENGE 02
BERWICK TO PAXTON HOUSE

Having much enjoyed our night in Berwick, we embarked on the journey up-river. Our destination: Paxton House. The starting point was from our previous night's accommodation at the Youth Hostel in Dewar's Lane Granary, housed in a spectacular restoration by the Berwick-upon-Tweed Preservation Trust of a derelict granary dating back to 1769 which incorporates a greater lean in its outer wall than the Tower of Pisa (Italy).

We retraced our previous day's steps back towards the New Bridge, but veered left onto the New Road. This a pedestrian pathway that follows the river for a mile upstream, and built after the Napoleonic Wars to provide work for unemployed service personnel. When passing under the Bridge, it's worth admiring the structure – when opened in 1928 by the then Prince of Wales (later King Edward VIII), this incorporated the longest concrete span in Britain.

Our departure into countryside began once passing under Robert Stephenson's spectacular railway bridge (the Royal Border Bridge), opened by Queen Victoria in 1850. The image of the bridge with its dramatic and innovative coloured light display is well worth an evening stroll when operational.

2 — 002 Bridge Illuminated (Michael Barron)

The Royal Border Bridge — opened by Queen Victoria in 1850 — is spectacular by day & breathtaking when lit at night.

2 — 003 The Whitewall

Immediately after this, you come across the remnants of Berwick Castle, which previously stood on the site of what is now the railway station. You travel under the foot of the fortifications at the bottom of the White Wall leading to the last vestiges of what was once a major Castle, the footpath descending the wall was once known as 'Breakneck Path' for obvious reasons.

2 — 004 Driftwood Sculpture

A few hundred metres further on, take in the amazing sculpture of a boat overlooking the Tweed - created entirely from driftwood extracted from the river. This is due to the ongoing work and efforts of an extremely talented young Berwick artist.

At the culmination of the New Road you pass a small cottage known locally as Chateau Pedro, and originally part of the Askew Estate. The main house (Castle Hills) was to be found down-river and halfway up the slope - 70+ years ago, this was the local maternity home where I came into the world. It has since reverted to a private dwelling.

2 — 005 Down-River to Berwick

2 — 006 Whiteadder Bridge

Beyond the cottage is a pedestrian bridge leading into woodland with a well-maintained gravel path which I am led to believe involved the Berwick Ramblers – they deserve recognition for their efforts. Further on, we diverted left onto a more rustic path down to the river. The image looking down stream helps identify our journey up to that point.

The next leg followed the river upstream and involved traversing the main A1 trunk road, which bypassed Berwick in 1983 and involved the construction of an additional bridge. A short distance beyond entails crossing the Whiteadder (a tributary of the Tweed) via a pedestrian bridge. Prior to the provision of this, a crossing would have necessitated a diversion up-river to a modern bridge replacing the original stone example which was swept away by the devastating floods of 1948.

2 — 007 Fishing Shiel

2 — 008 West Ord

On your journey to Paxton House, you will encounter various small stone structures adjacent to the Tweed. These were 'Fishing Shiels,' and for centuries a vital aspect of the local economy (salmon fishing). In my lifetime this employed a great many people, but now the last surviving netting station is at the mouth of the river. The Paxton House Trust has a limited season of catching, tagging and releasing salmon – brilliant to watch when possible.

Before Paxton House, on the opposite river bank (in England) can be seen an imposing house with an interesting history. West Ord House was built in the early 1700s for Sir William Blackett's mistress Margaret Orde. His relatives were unaware of this until his death in 1756, when he bequeathed his estate to Sir Walter Calverley (his nephew) on condition he marry Elizabeth Orde (Sir William & Margaret's illegitimate daughter) and change his name to Blackett.

If you look beyond West Ord House way up on the ridge, hidden in the trees is Longridge Towers: once the stately home of Lord and Lady Jerningham (the Lady depicted in the statue encountered on Bank Hill), who in their day were major local landowners. It is now a thriving school.

West Ord House was built in the early 1700s.

09 Paxton House Grounds

010 Paxton Hide

Paxton House's grounds are entered from the east. Investigate the woodland circuit; something worth adding to your itinerary. There is much to engage with prior to visiting the beautifully proportioned neo-Palladian stately mansion. Follow the trail upriver via an avenue of trees and you come across the Boathouse. Continue on the river path and divert uphill a little later (passing an eclectic sculpture) to pay your dues at the shop within the big house.

2 — 012 Kingfisher

2 — 013 Sculpture

2 — 014 Water Wheel

Prior to so doing, and while walking along the riverbank, keep your eyes peeled for wildlife. Over the years I've been lucky enough to observe otter and their kits, as well as a flash of blue denoting a kingfisher – memorable. The Paxton House Trust has conveniently provided a bird hide further up-river to assist with the observation of such.

Before explaining more in relation to Paxton House, it is worth investigating some of the other interesting elements to be found within the grounds. The horse-gin, waterwheel, beam pump and hydram demonstrate how Paxton House was a pioneer in relation to the provision of running water to a big house. A fascinating information panel highlights local Border engineers who later became leading acolytes in relation to the Industrialisation of Britain.

2 — 015 Gingerbread House

2 — 016 Edinburgh Window

The Paxton House Trust has conveniently provided a bird hide further up-river to assist with the observation.

Other points of interest appertain to what we refer to as the 'Gingerbread House,' due to this being hidden in the woods. Look for the full-sized sculpture of a dog on the chimney. Just beyond, check out the 'Edinburgh Window.'

2 — 017 Paxton House

2 — 018 Picture Gallery (Jim Gibson)

A beautifully proportioned neo-Palladian Adam building, home to Chippendale furniture of major importance and artworks from the National Galleries of Scotland.

However, the star of the show is the House itself. Their guide book does an excellent job in highlighting its many points of interest: A beautifully-proportioned neo-Palladium Adam building with a Chippendale furniture collection of major importance, spectacular original artworks augmented by a magnificent picture gallery, with further artwork on loan from the National Galleries of Scotland. I will leave you to investigate – Paxton House is a gem with a fascinating history.

The house has a further aspect of interest, and worth checking out: The Ellem Fishing Club Exhibition. This is a celebration of the 'Oldest Active Fishing Club in the World,' as recorded in the Guinness Book of Records, which was formed by a group of Edinburgh and Berwickshire Gentlemen in 1829. It would be remiss not to point out that my father became a member in 1937 and remained so until his death in 2008 (at 71 years) - though he was not the longest-serving member.

We finish day two by pointing out our accommodation on this occasion: a campervan within Paxton House's well-appointed campsite. Also, there was our excellent meal at 'The Cross Inn,' which involved taking a short stroll to the village.

TWEED TRAIL CHALLENGE 02
BERWICK TO PAXTON HOUSE

Authors & Books
Black Friday – Peter Aitchison

A fascinating book I came across relating to the Eyemouth fishing disaster of 1881, when 189 men and boys were lost due to a hurricane which devastated the Berwickshire coast. This was a harrowing tale of tragedy, with an interesting insight to past and present generations of Paxton House owners (the Homes) and their involvement with Eyemouth, from burning witches to bitter legal battles with the Church of Scotland - which had a bearing on the number of lives lost.

Musicians & Popular Music
Fix You – Coldplay

Having just heard of the death of our great Aussie mate (The Doc) who succumbed to Mesothelioma after nine years. The song is apt reference - a moving performance at the funeral of a friend's inspirational grandson, also to cancer.

Composers & Classical Music
Vangelis – Chariots of Fire

On our walk to The Cross Inn, we noticed a panel on the church gate commemorating Mary Jane Reddin. She was the mother of Eric Liddell: a Gold Medallist at the 1928 Paris Olympics, as immortalised in the 1981 film *Chariots of Fire*.

Fine Wine
2020 Bourgogne Chardonnay, Domain Paul Pillot, Burgundy (France)

Another excellent wine recommendation from our son (Simon) proved perfect with our meal at The Cross Inn. I should explain this was taken from our cellar plan and corkage duly charged – a favoured method to ensure wines hit the mark.

Horncliffe by Ollie Cowgill

TWEED TRAIL CHALLENGE 03
PAXTON TO HORNCLIFFE

The Next Leg from Paxton to Horncliffe involved returning to the river trail and exiting the Paxton House grounds. To your right (half way along the riverside path) is Tweedhill House, an impressive stone villa. A local worthy (George Brown) many years ago informed me that his relative built the house on proceeds obtained from Australia's Gold Rush.

On the opposite bank at the top of the hill is a more recently-built dwelling. I am led to believe the original building (a ruin, and where we played when I was a youngster) was at one time owned by Jock (White Hat) Willis of the Cutty Sark clipper ship fame - who originated from Eyemouth, not far up the coast from Berwick-upon-Tweed.

A spectacular structure, which has recently undergone a total nut and bolt restoration.

Up-river from this point, and dominating the skyline, is the Union Chain Bridge. A spectacular structure, which has recently undergone a total nut and bolt restoration as highlighted by the imagery – having been totally taken apart, removed and subsequently reassembled. The result is truly exceptional, and brings to mind a modern sculpture.

3 — 003 Chainbridge Construction

3 — 004 Chainbridge

3 — 005 Chainbridge

The bridge was built in 1820, and is now 200+ years old! This the first suspension bridge in the world to handle vehicular transport

It is worth remembering that the bridge was built in 1820, and is now 200+ years old! This the first suspension bridge in the world to handle vehicular transport (as recorded in the Guinness Book of Records), and led the way for all the many subsequent structures found around the Globe. The Friends of the Union Chain Bridge deserve recognition.

The full-size sculpture of Captain Samuel Brown (RN) is a fitting tribute to a true pioneer of his age and found on English soil, the dog at his feet (Sassy) being our walking companion. A further sculpture is located on the opposite bank (on Scottish soil) and features a young civil engineer with her iPad, who worked on the recent restoration.

A few titbits of information: The Bridge replaced a dangerous ford and ferry service. The cost was £7,700.00. A stone bridge (at that time) would have cost in excess of £20,000.00. It took exactly one year to build. The design and engineering incorporated into the structure was truly revolutionary, and attracted the likes of Brunel and Telford.

There is much to cogitate on while crossing from Scotland into England. To learn more, Paxton House has an exhibit aimed at highlighting the history and restoration of the bridge. Also once, in England, veer off the Tweed Trail and follow the road uphill for quarter of a mile and you will find The Honey Farm which also has information relating to the bridge.

The bridge's revolutionary design & engineering took just one year to complete.

3 — 006 Captain Brown

3 — 008 Honey Bee (Paul Herron)

The Honey Farm is a fascinating family-run enterprise going back four generations. Marvel at the wide range of products generated from the humble honey bee. Also, witness the eclectic assortment of farm implements highlighting the advancements in agriculture over the years. An unexpected sight relates to a London bus which houses their café. Also, while at the Honey Farm, take in 'Kath's Garden' - a tribute to a special lady who left her mark in multiple ways.

3 — 007 I-Pad Sculpture

3 — 009 Honey Farm Cafe

3 — 010 Grinham's Wood

Returning to the footpath, a signpost is soon to be erected for 'Benchmark at Grinham's Wood.' This is a local initiative to highlight the 'Grinham Legacy' and celebrate a Horncliffe couple who left their mark. Pierrette survived her husband Fredrick and, on her death, her French relatives generously donated the proceeds of the estate to the village.

3 — 011 Paths

'Benchmark at Grinham's Wood' aims to recognise their generosity and promote Paths & Benches; Woodland & Wildlife; History & Commemoration; Art & Photography; and Health & Wellbeing. Follow the Lower Tweed Trail to Horncliffe and a mile beyond to learn more. This is a fascinating insight into a small village perched high above the Tweed.

3 — 012 River View

Benchmark at Grinham's Wood celebrates the Grinham Legacy — a gift that supports paths, wildlife, history, art, & wellbeing.

3 — 013 Cockburn's Bench

The 'Benchmark' element relates to past members of the community and their involvement as teenagers in World War II. Each bench is dedicated to an individual family's memory. Hence 'Health & Wellbeing,' and the reference earlier in the book as to 'A Thought for the Youth of Today & Yesterday'. To learn more turn, to the book's later chapters.

3 — 014 Fishing Shiel Memorial

A further commemorative aspect of the initiative is their plans for a Fishing Shiel Memorial, designed to recognise a way of life once intrinsic to the local economy and entwined with village life. Many of those returning home after their wartime service resumed salmon fishing via coble and net - hence the repurposing of a derelict fishing station into a viewing platform with an information panel highlighting the shiel's past function and purpose.

3 — 015 Horncliffe House

When at 'Grinham's Wood,' you will see to your left - on the hill - an imposing stately mansion named Horncliffe House. It was built in 1800 by William Alder (who, by chance, is a distant relative of mine). A later custodian, Mr Allan - who, along with his brother, were the founders of Allan Bros, a longstanding Berwick company - was also related to my family by marriage.

The Grinham Legacy funded the restoration of the war memorial, honouring those lost in WWI and WWII.

Relating back to Annie, Lady Jernigham's statue, it's worth pointing out that until 1920 much of Horncliffe and the surrounding land (3,240 acres) was owned by the Jerninghams. The village at that time was a hive of activity with a farm, pub, smithy, joiners and undertakers, builders, market garden, tailors, two shops, church and salmon fishing. A number of these properties were sold at this time, when the estate went to public auction on the death of Lord Jernigham.

Today, Horncliffe involves a much quieter and genteel way of life - the Fishers Arms being the only commercial operation.

As you continue on the path to Horncliffe (England's most northerly village), hidden from view on the opposite bank (except when leaves are off the trees) are the remnants of a church and graveyard. Horncliffe Church never possessed such, hence most burials taking place at Norham. Some, however, were ferried across the river to Scotland and buried at Fishwick Church. The last funeral held there was in 1912 for a Lady McBriar of Hutton.

In relation to the community project 'Benchmark at Grinham's Wood,' it is important to point out the restoration of the war memorial - recording those who lost their lives during WW1 and WW2 - was financed via the Grinham Legacy. Sgt David T. Davidson (RAF) lost his life during WW2, and is recorded on the war memorial. Added to this is soon to be a commemorative bench and plinth on the riverside path, paying tribute to him and recording an element of his story.

To finish: Our accommodation in Horncliffe (The Fishers Arms) deserves mention, as this was recently purchased and renovated by the local community - having raised well in excess of £300,000.00. An amazing effort for a small village, and an example to others. The food, wine and room proved excellent, and the local bonhomie was very much in evidence.

3 — 018 War Memorial

3 — 019 Fishers Arms

TWEED TRAIL CHALLENGE 03
PAXTON TO HORNCLIFFE

Authors & Books
The Last Heroes – Gary Bridson-Daley

Many of Horncliffe's young residents enlisted or were called up during the Second World War and joined the likes of the Royal and Merchant Navy, Army and Air Force. 'The Last Heroes' incorporates 58 poignant and thought-provoking interviews with veterans who survived the conflict, and focuses on the telling of their stories. Various of these accounts directly relate to what these village forebears encountered, most of them mere teenagers at the time.

Musicians & Popular Music
Eric Clapton – Tears In Heaven
(also version by 3 Choir Boys)

'Benchmark at Grinham's Wood' aims to celebrate and highlight a prior generation who went through unimaginable trials and tribulations to enable us (hopefully) never to follow in their footsteps. Hence this rendition of 'Tears in Heaven' is apt in remembering those who are no longer with us, and their gift to future generations.

Composers & Classical Music
Fanfare For The Common Man – Aaron Copland

American composer Aaron Copland produced this work in 1942 during WW2 – and, as alluded to in the title, 'Fanfare for the Common Man' was aimed at all the many unsung combatants who took part in this devastating conflict.

Fine Wine
2007 Hospice de Beaune, Mazis-Chambertin Grand Cru, l'élevage Albert Bichot, Burgundy (France)

A special bottle of wine presented to me by a great friend (the Laird), and apt in relation to drinking a toast to the past Stalwarts of Horncliffe. I must also record that our meal and accommodation at the Fishers Arms proved excellent.

Norham Castle by Ollie Cowgill

TWEED TRAIL CHALLENGE 04
HORNCLIFFE TO NORHAM

After my farther's death in 2008 my two sisters, brother and I donated a bench and created an observation platform taking in a view much loved by our parents, and where as children - along with other members of our community - we would go to observe the fishermen cast their nets (a shot) from the fishing shiel on the opposite bank. A number of years later, this acted as a catalyst and element in the creation of the 'Benchmark at Grinham's Wood' project.

3 — 002 Horncliffe Up-River

The first mile of your journey from Horncliffe to Norham encompasses the second half of the 'Benchmark at Grinham's Wood' initiative, and incorporates spectacular views up-river to St Thomas's Island (better known locally as the 'Bat Island'). As you leave the village, you come across a sign for 'Herriot's Walk' – an honour bestowed on my parents by Horncliffe Parish Council in recognition of their efforts and involvement in the community over many years.

3 — 003 Glen

3 — 004 St Thomas' Island

3 — 005 Horncliffe Down-River

A short distance further on, you cross a stream emanating from 'The Glen' - a steep-sided valley, once a much-favoured walk. This dates back to when the railway station at 'Velvet Hall' was in operation, and people would come by train from Berwick and further afield to enjoy what was a spectacular promenade. The Glen's flora and fauna, along with the Mill, are recorded in postcards from a bygone era. As a child, this amenity was still much utilised and cherished by the village community.

On the stream's opposite bank, you come across a set of 73 extremely steep steps bringing you out way above the river - with truly breath-taking vantage points. The memorial benches along this stretch of the 'Grinham's Wood' project have spectacular views both up and down river. It's worth bearing in mind that the path you are following was once the daily commute for countless fishermen over centuries - and still operational as such when I was a child.

It would be remiss not to highlight one of the aims of the 'Grinham's Wood' initiative: the promotion of Woodland and Wildlife. The 25 acres of river bank and Glen, as well as those down river to the Union Chain Bridge, are a haven for wildlife. Over the years I've observed otter, deer, badgers, foxes, etc. There has also been a multitude of birds: Kingfishers, sand martins, swans, owls, woodpeckers - more recently, and unusually, an osprey; also egrets.

4 — 007 Woodpecker

4 — 008 Badger

4 — 009 Up-River

Swans are regular visitors — watching them take off from the water is a sight to behold.

While walking high above the river bank and with reference to woodland, look out for 'Stalwarts' Copse,' which is planned to incorporate a variety of native trees and being planted as a tribute to those from the local community who served their country during the Second World War, and to mark the 80th anniversary of the ending of the conflict.

This image from a little further on aptly demonstrates wildlife in action, and something you are likely to encounter. Swans are regular visitors - watching them come into land or take off from water is a sight to behold. A tad beyond, you may be lucky enough to catch a glimpse of an unusual herd of cattle – an ancient breed (Longhorns).

The next section of the walk to Norham follows the river at a lower level and passes a number of old fishing shiels with one now repurposed for salmon fishing via rod and line, rather than traditional net and boat. Fly fishing is an important aspect and contributor to the River Tweed's economy, providing work and jobs for a wide array of people.

013 Up-River to Castle

The river curves gently to the left, bringing into view an imposing spectacle: the remains of Norham Castle. As you walk upstream, you gain an insight as to what a formidable fortification this must have been in its heyday. The path, running alongside the outer wall, is steep and undulating - it lends awareness in relation to those poor souls engaged in besieging or capturing the castle. To enter the grounds requires going beyond and returning uphill via the road.

The river curves gently to the left, bringing into view an imposing spectacle: the remains of Norham Castle.

4 — 014 Castle Entrance

The history of Norham Castle goes back in excess of 900 years and, in its day, was a vital aspect of defending the English/Scottish border. It was besieged on numerous occasions, and changed hands similarly. It overlooked a fording point on the river, and its situation on the border related to its importance and the extent of the immense fortifications.

Norham Castle's history spans over 900 years, standing as a vital defence.

As can be seen from the imagery, the remnants of this great Castle are still impressive and provide a sense of the scale required to defend what was, for many years, a highly strategic position. Norham Castle's demise came about in the reign of Elizabeth I, who refused further investment. It subsequently fell into a state of ongoing decline.

To learn more about Norham Castle, a book to read is Norham Castle by Lord Hubert Jerningham of Longridge Towers. The Castle was part of the estate during his tenure - something I learnt from the 1920 documentation associated with the Public Auction of Longridge Estate. It's apt to highlight the Jerninghams' involvement as, in their time, they played a major role in relation to much of the Lower Tweed.

4 — 015 Norham Castle

Worth investigation is an interesting information board in the outer ward relating to J.M.W. Turner (the renowned British artist) and his fascination with painting Norham Castle. During his lifetime, he completed six different works incorporating the Castle. The image of Norham Castle in winter provides an insight as to why this so intrigued him.

4 — 016 Winter Norham Castle

J.M.W. Turner painted Norham Castle six times — captivated by its beauty in every season.

In relation to history and antiquity, Norham has a further building of note - St Cuthbert's Parish Church. As the name implies, this has hosted Saints as well as Kings and Queens. At one stage, Robert the Bruce utilised the building as his headquarters, and in later times Cromwell trashed the building, which bears the scars to this day. Well worth a visit, as is delving into its interesting past. When in St Cuthbert's, search for a plaque recognising Daniel Logan Laidlaw VC – 'The Piper of Loos'. He was the recipient of the highest and most prestigious award for gallantry available for an act of truly outstanding courage and heroism.

A point of pilgrimage in Norham's graveyard for those wishing to celebrate the Grinhams, and their French relatives' amazing generosity, may well be the recently-restored headstone marking the grave of Pierrette and Fredrick. Without them, 'Benchmark at Grinham's Wood' would not have come about and available to those partaking of this.

4 — 017 Norham Church

Norham incorporates a quintessential village scene involving an eclectic range of houses lining the wide main street.

4 — 018 Norham Green

Norham incorporates a quintessential village scene involving an eclectic range of houses lining the wide main street - leading to a central village green and its prominent medieval cross. When on the green looking back towards the castle, you will see an information panel depicting a further Turner painting. One building in particular left an impression - the recently-restored 'Victoria Inn,' where we quenched our thirst, ate an excellent meal, and spent a comfortable night. Also worth mentioning is Foreman's the butcher (immediately opposite), where we replenished our supplies.

TWEED TRAIL CHALLENGE 04
HORNCLIFFE TO NORHAM

Authors & Books
Wildlife In The Balance – Simon Mustoe

My great friend, the Aussie Doc (mentioned earlier), and our wives shared many magical mystery tours together. He and I talked at great length, from which I learnt much. This was a book he presented me with on our most recent (and, sadly, final) meeting. The message contained within, in relation to wildlife and our planet, is extremely enlightening.

Musicians & Popular Music
Wish You Were Here – Pink Floyd

This entry is possibly a tad melancholy – but a piece of music which takes Debbie and I back a great many years. The mention and remembrance of my much-loved parents, and the Doc brought about the sentiment in relation to the title.

Composers & Classical Music
Be Curious – Steve Luck (sometimes referred to as Newcastle's answer to Why/Einaudi)

Music which appeared to fit the bill in relation to sitting up high overlooking the river and island below, as well as taking in the magnificent vista beyond, and looking out for wildlife which the 'Grinham's Wood' project encapsulates. Steve is a talented Geordie composer whom we met at a recent art fair in Newcastle - and were impressed.

Fine Wine
2007 Taittinger Comtes de Champagne Blanc de Blanc (France)

A vintage champagne to toast our great Aussie mate (Kik) who, a few weeks previously, invited us to Oz for 'The Kik Off' – his living funeral. Sadly he succumbed prior to the big day – which nonetheless turned into a memorable memorial.

Kingfisher by Ronnie Hek

TWEED TRAIL CHALLENGE 05
NORHAM TO CORNHILL

This next leg of the challenge involves turning right after exiting the Vic and retracing the previous day's steps (parallel to the village green), followed by a further right turn heading towards the church and churchyard - but in this instance, continue down the lane bringing you out at the river.

On reaching the river, the Lower Tweed Trail goes left - but we would recommend a brief detour to your right to take in an impressive vista portrayed in a further Turner painting 'Norham Castle on the Tweed, Summer's Morn.' An information panel provides additional detail.

A striking avenue of poplar trees, planted in 2005 by local residents, lines the path to the stone bridge.

Quarter of a mile up-river, you come across an impressive stone bridge. Prior to this, the path incorporates a striking avenue of poplar trees planted in 2005 by an enterprising group from the local community. Another fine example of residents from a small village leaving their mark on the future.

Norham Bridge deserves mention: this stone edifice was opened in 1877, replacing a previous timber trestle structure which must have been impressive in its day, but obviously not up to the force of the river Tweed. It lasted a mere 48 years, compared to the current structure's 138 years and counting.

5 — 003 Norham Bridge Down-Stream

5 — 005 Ladykirk Church

Ladykirk Church was built by King James IV of Scotland in thanks for his survival during the siege of Norham Castle in 1496.

5 — 004 Microlight Image

The Lower Tweed Trail then follows the path below the bridge, but before doing so we suggest a further detour. This involves crossing the bridge into Scotland: first to take in the spectacular views (both up and down river), and secondly to visit Ladykirk's unusual historic church. It involves approximately a mile and a quarter round trip, aptly demonstrated by my image taken from a microlight – but it's worth the effort.

Ladykirk Church was constructed on the orders of King James IV of Scotland after he almost drowned while fording the Tweed during the siege of Norham Castle in 1496. His belief being that the Virgin Mary saved his life, hence the decision to build what is a magnificent church for such a small rural parish.

When returning to the bridge and crossing back into England, a right turn is required to bring you onto the Lower Tweed Trail. But in so doing, you will miss an element that's a great favourite of our young grandchildren: they love going under the arch of the bridge and shouting as loud as they possibly can. The subsequent echo is dramatic and greatly amuses them.

5 — 006 Bird Hide

5 — 007 Kingfisher

The trail from this point follows the river and subsequently joins the road (Boat House Lane) which brings you back onto the riverside path heading in the direction of Newbiggin Dean. Here you will find a well-placed bird hide incorporating some fascinating pictures demonstrating the native wildlife.

This next phase follows the river and, at the time of our journey, was decidedly overgrown. But persevere, as this brings you out into a magical woodland setting. Prior to this, look out for a small cylindrical building with a conical roof on the opposite bank - this is a novel fishing shiel on the Ladykirk Estate.

5 — 008 Fox

5 — 009 Ladykirk Fishing Shiel

A winding path through ancient woodland is good for the soul. To hear the wind rustling the leaves, branches groaning and the sun glinting through the trees provides a tonic to one's everyday life.

5 — 010 Woodland Walk

The latter part of the path through the woods rises way above the river, and provides a view through the overhanging branches to a further cylindrical shiel now repurposed as a fishing hut on the opposite bank. This belongs to the Milne-Graden Estate, whose magnificent mansion was built for Admiral Sir David Milne in 1823. It has a fascinating history and, if you read 'Black Friday' as featured in the 'Berwick to Paxton House' chapter, you will learn how intertwined the families of Milne-Graden and Paxton House became.

5 — 011 Milne Graden Fishing Hut

The woodland path comes out onto the now-defunct Tweedmouth-Kelso-St Boswells railway line involved in the Beeching closures of the 1960s. This next section of the Lower Tweed Trail follows the railway line - but, once again, we propose an additional detour downhill to your right.

5 — 012 Cliff at Tillmouth

The track to the river comes out at a further shiel, now repurposed as a fishing hut, not cylindrical on this occasion but of two storeys - which is unusual. On the opposite bank is a steep cliff; I was once lucky enough to watch two young peregrine falcons fly the nest for the first time from way up on the cliff face.

The track to the river comes out at a further shiel, now repurposed as a fishing hut.

5 — 013 Peregrine

5 — 014 Tillmouth Viaduct

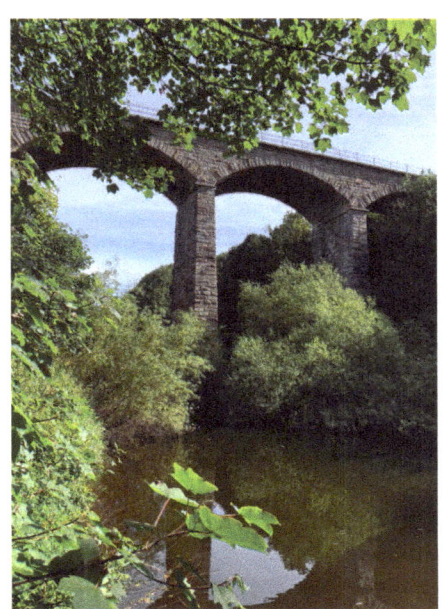

Follow the river upstream and you come across the confluence of the Tweed and Till - an impressive sight. Our suggested diversion requires a trip along the Till, whereupon you come across a magnificent railway viaduct, aptly demonstrating the infrastructure involved in the Victorian railway era.

Continue on the path up river and under Twizell Viaduct, and you come to another much earlier bridge. This was built in 1511 and, for three centuries, possessed the longest single span of any bridge in Britain. Twizell Bridge played a pivotal role in the defeat of Scotland's army by the English forces at Flodden Field.

Built in 1511 and, for three centuries, possessed the longest single span of any bridge in Britain.

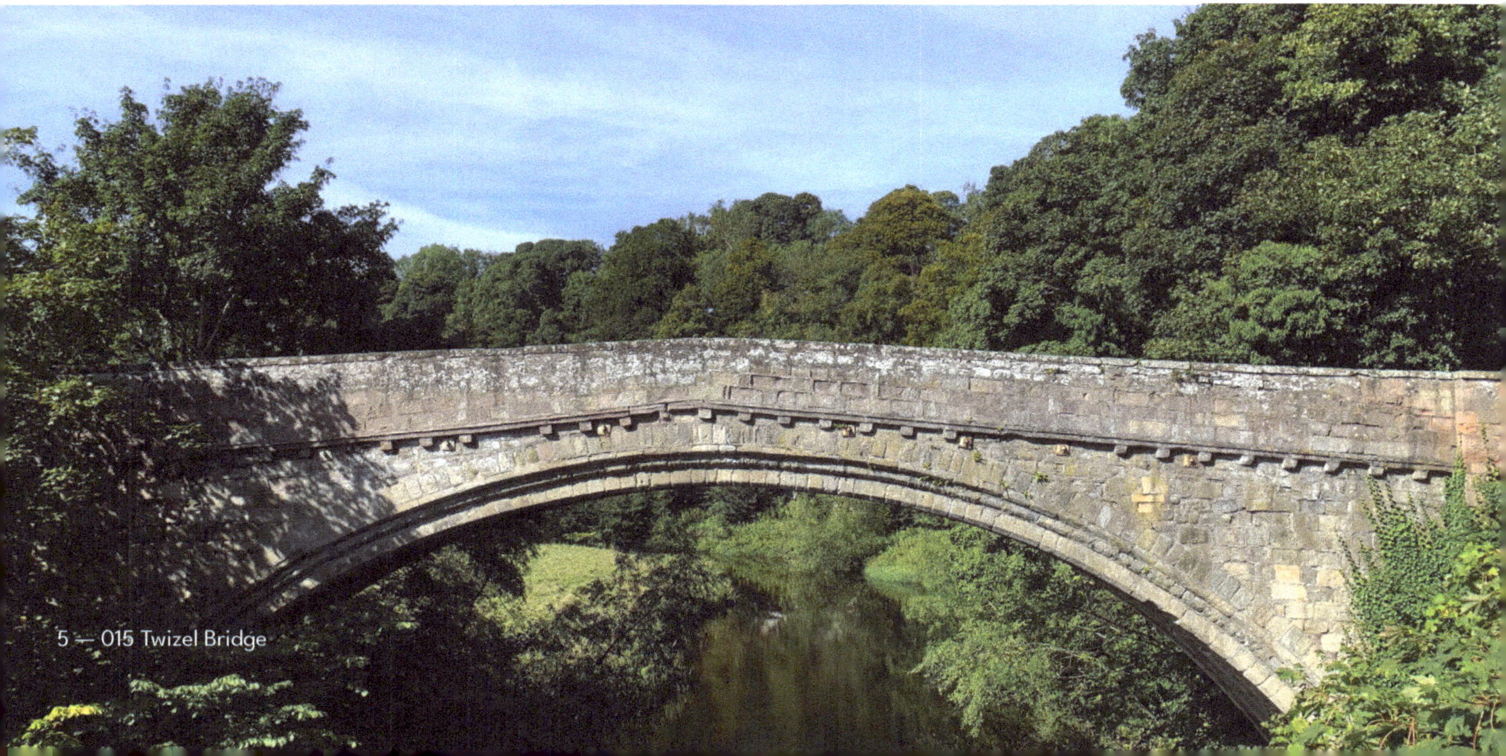

5 — 015 Twizel Bridge

5 — 016 Twizel Folly

When on the bridge looking downstream, hidden in the trees above the cliff are the remnants of what was originally a medieval tower house. Around 1770 this was remodelled on an enormous scale as a Gothic revival mansion by Sir Francis Blake. It was never completed and later turned into a folly, with much of the stone utilised to construct Tillmouth Park - a stately mansion situated up-river on the opposite bank.

Our diversion involves an uphill walk to the folly and then to a road, beyond which brings you back to the railway line that you follow out onto Twizel's Railway Viaduct - which provides amazing vistas of the Till, with a further folly encountered downstream: St Cuthbert's Chapel.

The next leg involves a right turn immediately beyond the viaduct and downhill to the river. Your route then skirts a field with very little path in evidence, and onwards to what in comparison is a major roadway – sadly much of this is without a river view. Eventually you will come upon the river, which provides some excellent vantage points of what appear to be significant Tweed salmon fishing beats.

Beyond this, the path goes inland and no longer follows the river. Instead, it heads towards Donaldson's Lodge, at which point we met the main Cornhill road and subsequently re-joined the public footpath heading west. We then lost the trail and came across another bridge crossing the defunct railway line.

We gamely ploughed on after relocating the path, and came out short of Coldstream Bridge - much of this without sight of the river, other than the final section. This involved following a meandering track through a more recently constituted woodland, with glimpses of the river through the trees. The foresight of those responsible for the tree planting deserve mention.

On reaching the A697, we headed south to Cornhill and our abode for the night – The Collingwood Arms.

TWEED TRAIL CHALLENGE 05
NORHAM TO CORNHILL

Authors & Books
Some Other Rainbow – John McCarthy & Jill Morrell

When entering 'Benchmark at Grinham's Wood' from the Chain Bridge, you encounter a small, glazed post box-like structure full of books, which is where I came across Some Other Rainbow. It's an amazing story of two people – one held hostage for five and a half years by the Islamic Jihad in Lebanon, and the other's efforts to have him freed. If your world is getting on top of you, learn how others cope in extreme adversity.

Musicians & Popular Music
Bridge Over Troubled Water – Simon & Garfunkel

This leg of the trail encounters a number of bridges with several of them crossing water – hence 'Bridge Over Troubled Water' seemed apt to accompany us on this particular leg of our Lower Tweed Trail journey. The song takes us back a great many years (to our youth), and seems relevant in relation to the book choice.

Composers & Classical Music
Rhapsody In Blue – George Gershwin

As the imagery portrays, the sky was blue for much of the day - hence 'Rhapsody in Blue' appeared to fit the bill. Plus we deemed the rise and fall of tempo within the music apt in relation to the wide and diverse range of landscapes, structures, history and anecdotes encountered along the way.

Fine Wine
2023 Whispering Angel, Côtes de Provence Rosé (France)

A rosé was deemed appropriate, as it had been such a glorious day. Hence a chilled glass seated in the Collingwood Arms' garden prior to dinner (basking in the late evening sunshine) seemed perfect, and an opportunity to discuss our Lower Tweed journey so far.

Coldstream Bridge by James Herriot

TWEED TRAIL CHALLENGE 06
COLDSTREAM

The views from Coldstreams Bridge both up and down river are spectacular, and if there during the salmon fishing season you may be lucky enough (as we were) to watch an angler land a salmon. The bridge was opened in 1766 and, at that time, the only other one downstream was at the river mouth (Berwick-upon-Tweed) - a 40 mile round trip.

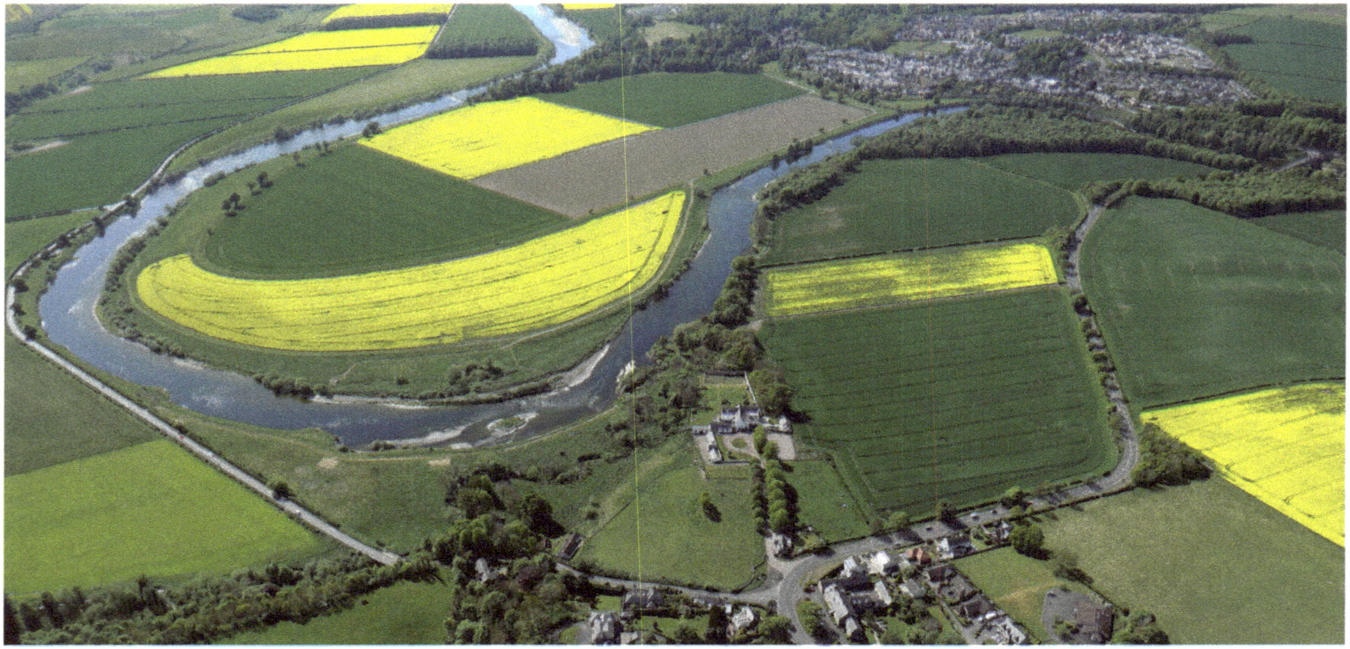

After a night's rest and recuperation at the Collingwood Arms (Cornhill) and an excellent breakfast served by their attentive staff, we were once more on our way. The Lower Tweed Trail officially ends at this point, but we highly recommend an addition to your journey whilst in the vicinity and explore Coldstream - being just over the border in Scotland. Hence us retracing our previous day's steps in the direction of Coldstream Bridge.

The Lower Tweed Trail officially ends at this point.

6 — 003 Marriage House

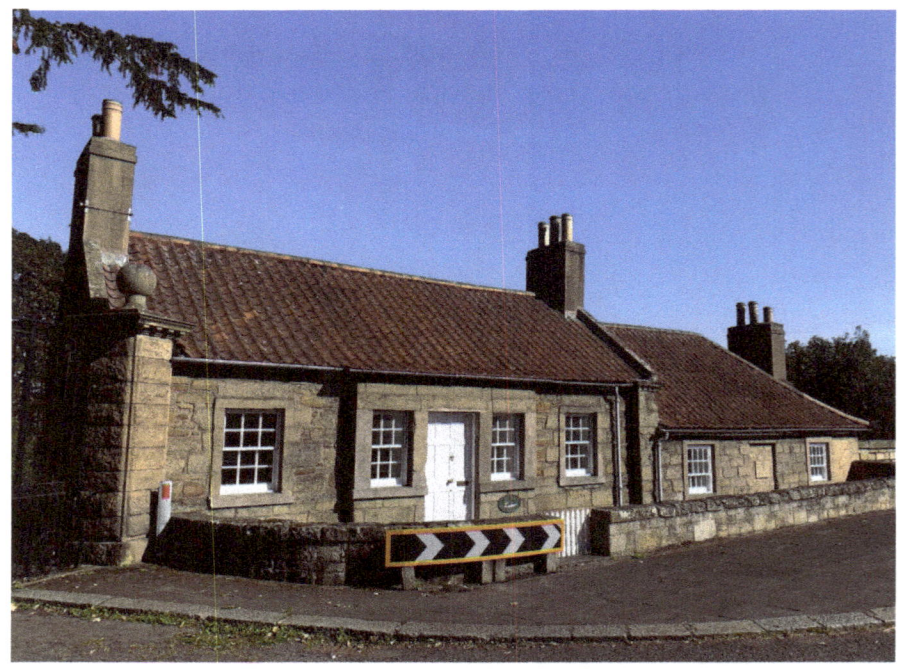

6 — 004 Lennel

6 — 005 Woodland

The Marriage House, once operating like Gretna Green.

The architect for the bridge was John Smeaton; another of his projects being the third Eddystone Lighthouse. The cost of the bridge was £6,000.00 and took a little over 3 years to build. An interesting aspect relates to the Toll House which, as you will see, is called the Marriage House which operated as per Gretna Green for many years in relation to runaway marriages.

Having seen little of the river Tweed on the latter part of the previous day, we decided to wander down-stream and view this from a Scottish perspective. The first building below the Marriage House is an extremely smart fishing hut – far more contemporary than any we'd previously encountered. Similarly, there was an equally elegant fishing establishment on the opposite bank.

Further down river, I made the faux pas of letting our companion Sassy (the dog) in for a swim – not realising anyone was fishing! On hearing expletives, I went to apologise and found the recipient was (only) the head of the Tweed Commissioners. He could not have been nicer, and we engaged in a fascinating conversation in relation to their work regarding salmon and riparian conservation.

At the end of the field following the river, we came across signs for a public path heading back to Coldstream. Initially this involved a fenced walkway through the middle of the field, from which we observed a building of interest peeking through the trees. This turned out to be Lennel House and, as we were to learn from an information panel a little later, Robert Burns (Scotland's national bard) was entertained there at one time.

It turns out that Lennel has an interesting history, having been utilised during the First World War for convalescing officers – one such being an Australian recipient of the Victoria Cross. A further snippet was gained relating to Beatrix Potter once having holidayed with her family at Lennel House. Our knowledge of this stately mansion (now a care home) is limited, but deserves further investigation.

As you may have gathered, Debbie and I greatly enjoy walking the river banks, but I should add that woodland such as this - with sunlight on the trees - provides a touch of magic. Our woodland walk back into Coldstream (as demonstrated by the photographic evidence) was a case in point.

Our woodland walk back into Coldstream, with sunlight filtering through the trees, was pure magic.

6 — 006 Monument

On entering Coldstream, you come across an impressive monument to a past local MP - Charles Marjoribanks Esq. The inscription is interesting: To Perpetuate Their Admiration of His High Talents, Amiable Qualities and Political Principles. If true, today's cohort of MPs could learn from such sentiments.

6 — 007 Nuns Walk Down-Stream

6 — 008 Nuns Walk Up-Stream

Subsequent to the monument, we followed the path up-river on Nuns Walk, followed by Penitent's Way - indicating a religious affiliation, perhaps? It turns out that these relate back to the 12th century, when a Cistercian Priory was founded in the town and remained in existence until 1558. The nuns played their part in looking after the wounded and dying following the battle of Flodden Field. The views, as you can see, are spectacular.

Further along and to the left of Nuns Walk, you come across a memorial to the Battle of Flodden.

After Penitent's Way, we crossed a pedestrian bridge over the river Leet and followed the Tweed up-stream. This is a walk we've undertaken many times, and encompasses the famous Lees salmon fishing beat. The pair of us love to watch the salmon leaping clear from the water, and to observe those fishing for such. The book suggestion accompanying this section of our journey provides a powerful insight into this world.

6 — 009 Temple

6 — 010 Lees House

6 — 011 Hobbit House

The reason for the naming of the Temple Pool becomes obvious when you come across the folly situated adjacent to this. The Lees Estate once encompassed a substantial stately mansion, and an indication of a previous resident came from the plaque on the monument we'd observed earlier in the day: Charles Marjoribanks Esq MP, the son of Sir Charles Marjoribanks-Bart of Lees.

The house was abandoned of habitation in the 1940s, and subsequently fell into dereliction. However, the current owners (the co-authors of this week's book) have since restored the central rotunda and later added the two wings, creating and restoring this to what is now a truly exceptional property.

Following the public footpath inland through the woods provides an excellent view of the house, and a little further on you come across what appears a Hobbit House with a tree on its roof - originally this was an ice-house.

Continue on the path and you come out at the far end of Coldstream, back to the A697, whence we took a left turn heading out of town, then immediately right into the Hirsel Estate. The monument as you enter the grounds provides an indication as to the current owners and their forbears.

Once abandoned and derelict, the House's central rotunda has been lovingly restored, transforming it back into an exceptional property.

Sir Alec Douglas-Home was the Prime Minister of a Conservative administration during the 1960s and twice served as Foreign Secretary, and was also an aide to Neville Chamberlain during the time of the Munich Agreement (1938). Our chosen book provides an interesting insight to Sir Alec - the author being his nephew.

6 — 012 Sir Alec

The Hirsel Estate offers woodland walks, rich heritage, and exhibitions.

The Hirsel Estate is well worth visiting not only for the woodland and wildlife, but its buildings and heritage. Once again, it is a place we've visited on many occasions. In this case, our visit was in late summer, but I'd suggest returning (if possible) at different times of year to appreciate their outstanding scenery. Prior to walking the grounds, we stopped off for a well-earned coffee and tray-bake at their excellent tea-room.

The exhibition housed in the adjoining stable complex provides a fascinating insight to the Estate's past – plus an interesting photographic display which highlights the reason to visit throughout the seasons. There are also workshops involving an eclectic group of skilled craftspeople from the worlds of pottery, glass and stone carving.

6 — 013 House (Stephen Whitehorne)

6 — 014 Woods (Stephen Whitehorne)

6 — 015 Lake

6 — 016 Heron

As my image of the lake demonstrates, the wildlife that this environment and the woodlands provide is diverse. The bird hide further along the lake shore is an excellent location to sit quietly and observe such.

Dundock Wood's rhododendrons are a spectacular sight.

We traversed around the lake to Dundock Wood, which at the right time of year has the most spectacular display of rhododendrons. We subsequently passed the main house and continued to the Leet, crossing the bridge to the other bank and then following the path and drive back into Coldstream.

Our time in Coldstream was curtailed as time was marching on, but we had a wander around the streets and came across the Coldstream Museum in the Market Square, which explains the Coldstream Guards' association with the town. The impressive church and war memorial on the Main Street are further points of interest.

6 — 017 Deer

On our way back to the Collingwood Arms (Cornhill), we came across a sign to Jacob's Well, which proved to be slightly underwhelming. However, the view of Coldstream Bridge from this location was truly magical, as our final image demonstrates.

TWEED TRAIL CHALLENGE 06
COLDSTREAM

Authors & Books
A River Runs Through Me – Andrew Douglas-Home

For those wanting to better understand the world of salmon fishing, this an excellent book. It provides an interesting viewpoint and understanding in relation to river and country life. Regards the 'Youth of Today & Yesterday,' the author records his father spending 3.5 years as a Japanese prisoner of war, and his godfather being incarcerated in Colditz Castle by Hitler's Nazi regime - both as young men. There is more to the book than mere fishing - not least the telling of their own personal family tragedy and the consequences. It helps to put things in perspective.

Musicians & Popular Music
Perfect Day – Lou Reed

Perfect Day is totally appropriate to what proved to be exactly that – Coldstream providing so much more than expected, and hence our visit taking longer than we originally envisaged. It also takes us back a great many years.

Composers & Classical Music
Parce Mihi Domine – Christobal de Morales (Choir & Saxophone)

A haunting piece of music with religious connotations, hence apt in relation to Coldstream's past in relation to the Cistercian Priory and the nuns who inhabited this location from the 12th century.

Fine Wine
Dufouleur Père & Fils, Crémant de Bourgogne, Burgundy, NV (France)

It should have been vintage Champagne! But as I was supplying the wine for this illustrious event (explanation included in the next chapter), and knowing my friends would not hold back, I went for one of our favourites: a Cremant (a less expensive option) produced as per Champagne - but from a different region of France.

Stoat by Ronnie Hek

TWEED TRAIL CHALLENGE 07
CORNHILL

Our original intention was to include Cornhill along with Coldstream, and to celebrate the culmination of our exploration of the 'Lower Tweed' with a slap-up meal and suitable wines with 'Sabbatical Friends' at the Collingwood Arms. But as identified in the prior entry, Coldstream proved to have taken longer than originally envisaged.

Two new chapters — 'Bird's Eye View' and 'An Otter's Perspective' — were inspired by an evening of fine wine, good company, and lively conversation about our Lower Tweed adventures.

Hence the decision to investigate Cornhill the following morning prior to our departure – but without interrupting our festivities. Which, in themselves, brought about the addition of two further chapters to the book – being 'Birds Eye View' and 'An Otter's Perspective'.

These require explanation, as they came about due to the effects of copious quantities of excellent wine and bonhomie - as you would expect the chat related (in the main) to our 'Lower Tweed Experience' and the pleasure derived from this. The only slight regret related to not being in a position to see and follow the river throughout, which brought about a bizarre discussion as to wildlife having better access than us humans.

7 — 003 Barn Owl

Wildlife spotting along the Tweed sparked lively riverside debates.

As you will have gathered, an aspect of 'Tweed Trail Challenge' we greatly enjoyed relates to observing wildlife. This led to a debate as to which of these has the better access and view when following the river up-stream: salmon and trout were discussed, also swans, ducks, herons and other birds, alongside otters, foxes, deer and many more. This made for interesting deliberations once wine loosened the participants' tongues and inhibitions.

7 — 004 Fox & Cub

A further aspect to the dialogue related to having to be reasonably fit, as certain aspects of the trail would prove unsuitable for those with mobility issues. Hence the conversation expanded in relation as to how people with special needs or limited mobility could best access all we had so appreciated over the past week.

Discussions turned to how those with limited mobility could best enjoy the highlights of the Lower Tweed.

7 — 005 Buzzard

7 — 006 Stoat

7 — 006 Hot Air Balloon

7 — 008 Otter

7 — 009 Berwick Boat (Walter Baxter)

From hot air balloons to microlights, the best way to spot wildlife on the Tweed is up for debate.

The answers varied, and they included a hot air balloon, hovercraft, canoe, boat trips from Paxton House and Berwick, and even a flight in a microlight. The discussion investigated as to which of these best related to the various animals and birds involved in our earlier deliberations, and my personal wildlife preferences came down to an osprey and otter - with my chosen modes of transport to mimic what they would observe relating to microlight and canoe.

7 — 010 Osprey

7 — 012 Microlight

This led to my dinner colleagues proposing a series of wagers, with the proceeds going towards the coffers of the 'Benchmark at Grinham's Wood' initiative, if I was to take a flight in a microlight from the river mouth at Berwick-upon-Tweed to Cornhill and make the return journey via canoe - and subsequently report my findings to them in relation to an osprey and otter's point of view. As this was late in the evening and a drink or two on board, I foolishly accepted their challenge - hence the extra chapters.

A wager over wine set the microlight-to-canoe challenge in motion.

7 — 011 Canoe

7 — 013 Collingwood Arms

Returning to Cornhill, the Hotel's website has a scrap of information relating to the building's history.

The Collingwood Arms takes its name from the local merchant family which owned it until 1955. There are strong ties with Northumberland's 19th Century naval hero, Vice Admiral Cuthbert Collingwood, who served under Nelson around the time the hotel was built. Indeed our bedrooms take their names from the 15 ships in Collingwood's division at the battle of Trafalgar: -

HMS Royal Sovereign (Flagship), Bellisle, Mars, Tonnant, Bellerophon, Colossus, Achilles, Polyphemus, Revenge, Swiftsure, Defiance, Thunderer, Prince of Wales, Dreadnought and Defense.

Admiral Lord Collingwood's life is worth investigating. It's interesting to see he married Sarah Blackett: a family name which appeared in relation to West Ord House in the chapter 'Berwick-upon-Tweed to Paxton House'.

Cornhill House is an impressive residence, with its entrance and drive immediately to the west of the Collingwood Arms. It appears this building has history going back centuries prior to coming into ownership of the Collingwood family, having once been a fortified tower overlooking a river crossing (a ford) between England and Scotland – and involved in numerous military incursions, skirmishes, battles and wars over the years.

7 — 014 Cornhill House

Previous incumbents were illustrious Northumbrian landowning families: the Greys, Swinhoes and Fosters. I am no historian, and leave you to look into its fascinating background. But I would like to point out the current owners' amazing restoration of Cornhill House - which in 2014 was in dire need of a saviour. Their efforts, and those like them who take on such herculean tasks, deserve to be recognised and applauded.

7 — 015 War Memorial

7 — 016 Cornhill Shop

Having spent two nights at the Collingwood Arms, we became aware of the building to our left: the village shop and post office, which has been in existence since 1906. This amazing enterprise is obviously a much loved community institution and goes like a fair from dawn to dusk. The jovial and friendly team of ladies involved are an example to others in relation to customer service and looking after their wide and diverse clientele.

On our journey, each town and hamlet we've visited has had a War Memorial honouring those lost in both World Wars. Cornhill is no different, with 19 names recorded, which aptly emphasises the devastating impact these conflicts must have had on a small rural community. A snippet of information I gleaned relates to John Carnaby Collingwood of Cornhill House donating the land for the erection of the War Memorial in 1920.

7 — 017 Cornhill Church

7 — 018 Stain Glass Window

The church opposite aroused our curiosity, and hence an investigation. We learned that a church has apparently been on the site since Saxon times. The current example dates back to 1752. Local legend has it that during refurbishment in 1840, an 8ft-tall man was found buried under the nave. Also of note is the recent restoration of the magnificent East Window, created by Alfred Octavius Hemming in 1887. Other works of this eminent craftsman include the East Window of the Chapter House at Canterbury Cathedral, and the North Transept Window at Salisbury Cathedral.

Our final quest related to Coldstream Station which, bizarrely, was located a mile away and across the border in Cornhill. The rail line closed to passenger travel in 1964 and to freight transport in 1965. I was twelve years old and have fond memories of my Mum with my siblings in tow - attempting to outrun the 'Kelso Flyer' (a steam train) in her Morris Minor on our way to swimming lessons in Jedburgh. Happy times.

Sadly there is now little evidence of the original substantial station building with its two platforms, pedestrian bridge, signal box, turntable, engine shed, and sidings servicing the adjacent auction mart. A single buttress of the bridge crossing the A697 is now the only remnant and reminder of what was once a major transport hub.

During our brief exploration of Cornhill we came across an interesting cooperative ensconced in what was previously the village school – engaged with arts and crafts, as well as an opportunity to create one's own gin. Unfortunately, time not being on our side, it will have to await a return visit.

TWEED TRAIL CHALLENGE 07
CORNHILL

Authors & Books
Politics On The Edge – Rory Stewart

A fascinating insight to the dysfunction of politics in our country from a minister who served during a Conservative administration. My reason for including this relates to an earlier book by Rory (Border Marches), where he purports to have walked the border. My beef relates to no mention of Cornhill, Coldstream, Norham, Horncliffe or Paxton, with one meagre reference to Berwick-upon-Tweed being that of a meal.

Musicians & Popular Music
What a Wonderful World - Louis Armstrong

Having spent the last week exploring the delights of the Lower Tweed, 'What a Wonderful World' seemed to fit the bill perfectly. Debbie and I often comment on how lucky we are and pinch ourselves (metaphorically speaking). This adventure is right up there with the others, hence a fitting piece of music.

Composers & Classical Music
Tradition – Suo Gan - (Empire of the Sun) – Welsh Treble Chai Thomas

A traditional Welsh ballad utilised in Steven Spielberg's 1987 film 'Empire of the Sun'. The film is based on the book of the same name by J.G. Ballard, and tells his harrowing story as a young boy incarcerated in a Japanese prison camp during WW2. A pertinent reference to 'A Thought for the Youth of Today & Yesterday'.

Fine Wine
2020 Pavette, Pinot Noir, Napa Valley (California)

Home after a fairly full-on seven days, we were in need of a little rest and recuperation for both body and mind - consequently the decision to have steak and chips washed down with a suitable red wine. Debbie is no fan of heavy red wine, being more inclined to a dry white Burgundy - but can be tempted with an Aussie, New Zealand or Californian Pinot Noir, hence the choice.

TWEED TRAIL CHALLENGE 08
BIRDS-EYE VIEW

This being my first time in a microlight, what a day to choose – the weather was absolutely perfect, and I was able to see to the far horizon. As my imagery demonstrates, the panorama and perspective enjoyed by my chosen bird (an Osprey) is very different to that for us mere humans when plodding along the Lower Tweed. The aim and intention of this chapter is to provide an insight to what can be observed from way up high.

8 — 002 Pier & Berwick

Debbie, and my original trek (last year) from Berwick-upon-Tweed to Cornhill, took seven days - for my friend the Osprey, the journey time is under an hour. Looking down from 1,000 feet enables one to observe aspects totally unobtainable when on terra firma - an apt education as to the benefit of flight.

Having taken a mass of pictures during my microlight flight, I've reduced these down to a mere 15 - taking in various sections of our Lower Tweed journey, and in chronological order. My aim and intention was to point things out unavailable to Debbie and I when walking the river bank, but revealed from the air.

From 1,000 feet in a microlight, Berwick-upon-Tweed reveals its full grandeur – beaches, bridges, fortifications & river all in a panorama only available from the air

Berwick-upon-Tweed from the ground is an impressive place, but from the air one gets a bird's-eye view of the town's topography and layout. How the sea, beaches, river, bridges, pier, fortifications, open spaces, ancient and modern buildings all combine together as one is revealed. A vista that is normal and every-day to our feathered friends - but, except in special circumstances (such as a microlight flight), unavailable.

Approaching Berwick from the sea demonstrates the length of the pier, and emphasises the point made in the first chapter in relation to starting our 'River Tweed Odyssey' out in the North Sea. It also stresses the influence the river and the three iconic bridges play in relation to this ancient Border town. The further image highlights and demonstrates the scale and design of the Elizabeth fortifications - one of a kind in the United Kingdom.

This next image, going inland from the sea, incorporates the fourth bridge to cross the river Tweed. This is the most recent, and relates to the A1 truck road which bypassed the town in 1983. Beyond and to the right is the Whiteadder, a tributary of the Tweed - its pedestrian bridge points out the route of our Lower Tweed journey. Further up-river on the English bank can be seen West Ord House as featured in Chapter 2 (Berwick to Paxton).

A little further on, the imposing edifice of Paxton House comes into view, and the image aptly demonstrates the extent of the grounds and the delights this encapsulates, as highlighted earlier in the book. On the opposite bank can be seen one of the many fishing shiels encountered along our route.
In the right-hand corner is the village of Paxton, indicating its proximity to the Big House. A reminder of a pleasant evening spent with friends at the Cross Inn on the second leg of our Odyssey the previous year

The Osprey's view of an iconic structure: the Union Chain Bridge, as featured in the Guinness Book of Records and detailed in Chapter 3 (Paxton to Horncliffe). The Benchmark at Grinham's Wood section of the Lower Tweed Trail starts just beyond the bridge and onwards to Horncliffe and Grinham's Wood. To your left is a must-visit destination being the Honey Farm, with its fascinating collection of memorabilia.

8 — 006 Union Chainbridge

Horncliffe and its Stalwarts were the catalyst for the Benchmark at Grinham's Wood initiative, and the aerial view highlights the point made in Chapter 11 (The Village They Left Behind) as to this once being an isolated and self-sufficient community. One way in and a dead end, with the village unseen from the main road until the 1950s. Herriot's Walk is upstream from the village, and indicates the second section of Benchmark at Grinham's Wood, which culminates at St Thomas' Island (known locally as the Bat Island).

The walk up-river from the Bat Island takes in a couple of fishing shiels: The first of these is typical of how the majority of shiels looked in their heyday – small and functional. The second has been repurposed as a fishing hut in relation to salmon fishing by rod and line. Here there is competition for the Osprey, although with almost 100% catch and release they are returned to the river - so not off the menu for our feathered friends.

The bird's-eye view of Norham reveals its strategic castle, traditional village green, & broad main street — a layout shaped by centuries of history and defence.

The view of Norham from this angle and elevation highlights the strategic position of the castle, and the importance it once played in the defence of the realm. The bird's-eye view of Norham highlights its traditional layout, with a substantial and broad main street along with a central village green.

A further place of note we visited while in Norham on our Lower Tweed Trail journey the previous year was St Cuthbert's Parish Church – an impressive building with an interesting history. Another church discussed in the book is that of Ladykirk, which can be spotted on the Scottish bank of the river - off to your right. To get there requires a detour from the Trail, but it's well worth crossing the magnificent stone bridge to do so.

These next two images aptly demonstrate the advantage birds have in relation to the vistas and insight available to them. Earlier in the book, I utilised two images of circular buildings. I should point out these were originally fishing shiels, one now repurposed for fishing for salmon with rod and line. The point being that both are visible to those walking the Lower Tweed Trail – but the homes of those who own such are not.

My flight in the microlight provided an excellent view of the two estates, with their substantial houses belonging to those responsible for the two fishing shiels. The first being Ladykirk Estate, whose original stately home was sadly demolished and replaced in 1966. The second was that of Milne Graden, an impressive stately mansion with an interesting history in relation to various local aristocratic families and houses.

8 — 012 Till

This image encompasses the lower section of the River Till, a tributary of the Tweed. When following the Lower Tweed Trail, you cross the amazing Victorian railway viaduct - a great vantage point. Earlier in the book (Chapter 5 - Norham to Cornhill), we recommend a detour down to the Tweed and a walk along the Till under the viaduct and up-stream, looping back onto your original route - well worth doing.

8 — 013 Up-River to Coldstream

The Lower Tweed Trail unfortunately takes a detour inland towards Donaldson's Lodge at this juncture, meaning that the view of the river is sadly lost to us mere humans - but not so for the Osprey. The route comes out at Coldstream Bridge and, as highlighted earlier in the book, a further excursion is recommended by crossing the bridge and walking downstream to take in the view from the Scottish river bank.

8 — 014 Cornhill

The Lower Tweed Trail officially ends at Cornhill, but once again access via the river is denied - hence the final section involves following the A697 south to Cornhill. The aerial image of the village aptly demonstrates how the river sweeps around from Coldstream to Cornhill and back to Coldstream. The chapter on Cornhill provides an insight to the village, and the tale as to how I ended up in a microlight.

This final image demonstrates the juxtaposition of Cornhill and Coldstream - the latter not officially part of the Lower Tweed Trail, but a place worth adding to your itinerary. Hence the inclusion of a chapter on Coldstream within 'Tweed Trail Challenge,' which highlights aspects of this intriguing Border town.

A trip in a microlight taking in the view from an Osprey's perspective was fascinating and enlightening - providing vistas and insights not available to us humans when walking the Lower Tweed Trail. It raised funds and publicity for the 'Benchmark at Grinham's Wood' initiative – and I loved every minute of it.

8 — 015 Cornhill & Coldstream

TWEED TRAIL CHALLENGE 08
BIRDSEYE VIEW

Authors & Books
The Horse Boy – Rupert Isaacson

A further random book courtesy of the Union Chain Bridge book share post-box. This is a volume to make one comprehend the challenges of others and the lengths they are willing to undertake in finding a solution. The true story of a severely autistic boy and his parents, involving a trip to Outer Mongolia looking for answers to their situation. Provides an enlightening insight to diverse attitudes and approaches to life.

Musicians & Popular Music
Song For The Summer – Stereophonics

A favourite taken from Debbie's playlist and the lyrics are apt n relation to BAGW's statement reference 'A Thought for the Youth of Today & Yesterday,' and looking forward with an emphasis on 'Today & Tomorrow' rather than 'Yesterday'. A fitting song choice with reference to our Lower Tweed escapade.

Composers & Classical Music
The Lark Ascending – Ralph Vaughan Williams

I was unable to locate a piece of music relating to Ospreys, hence the decision to utilise a favourite by Vaughan Williams: 'The Lark Ascending'. This fits the bill in relation to flying in a microlight from Berwick-upon-Tweed to Cornhill and observing spectacular vistas from way on high (as seen from an Osprey's perspective). It's worth highlighting that Skylarks were regularly encountered on our Lower Tweed Trail adventure.

Fine Wine
2022, Bourgogne Blanc, Oncle Vincent, Olivier Leflaive, Burgundy (France)

Debbie's tipple of choice will always be a white Burgundy, which may well have something to do with our son - the 'Fine Wine Specialist' - as identified and explained in Chapter 13 being his 'Love Letter to Burgundy'. Plus our choice of wine in this instance has connotations in relation to Patsy and Eddie's (Debbie's) road trips through France!

Sand Martins by Ronnie Hek

9 — 001 Salmon

TWEED TRAIL CHALLENGE 09
AN OTTER'S PERSPECTIVE

My original thought as to creating imagery that demonstrates the views available to an Otter when swimming down the river Tweed from Cornhill to Berwick-upon-Tweed soon changed. Having canoed the river, I became aware many of the vistas are similar to what we humans observe from the river bank - with a couple of major differences. The first relates to unlimited access, with the second being the ability to observe wildlife. Plus a practical scenario not taken into account - paddling a canoe at the same time as taking amazing photographs is difficult.

I can vouch for the Otter having brilliant uninterrupted views - unlike us humans who at times (while walking the trail) would find them simply unavailable. An original aspiration had been to take pictures while travelling under the arches of each of the seven bridges en-route to Berwick. Unfortunately in most cases this required concentrating on the task in hand rather than that of taking pictures – fast water, stone parapets and cameras don't mix.

But it was the Otter's field of vision in relation to observing wildlife which was the real eye-opener. The perspective from the Osprey's point of view was amazing when flying high (in a microlight) way above the river – but that doesn't replicate the ability of both Otter and human to observe wildlife close at hand. Our canoe trip accentuated the fact that the Otter out in the river had a different vista in relation to humans walking the riverbank. Hence my decision to highlight the diversity of bird, fish and animal life encountered on our journey downstream.

The opening gambit took place just prior to canoeing under Coldstream bridge - this being a salmon leaping from the water. Due to the river being low, this was observed on only a few occasions. With all of our party being keen salmon fisher folk, this was something we delight in seeing. Our next encounter would take this to a different level..

Not long into our journey, what should appear above us but a pair of Ospreys! Truly spectacular to be in a position to observe them close up while in a canoe on the river. Having flown up-river in a microlight the previous week to gain an insight from an Osprey's perspective of the Lower Tweed Trail, it was an amazing opportunity to see them in action. Especially when the male caught a fish - a memorable 15 minutes while drifting downstream.

Seeing an Egret not that many years ago was an unusual sight – but not now. The first time I encountered one of these exotic birds on home turf was with a great friend, now sadly departed having dealt with cancer in an exemplary manner over an eleven year period. Whenever I see an Egret: Pauline (a very special person) immediately comes to mind, and our trip down the Tweed brought this to the fore.

9 — 004 Duck & Ducklings

An encounter with a mother Duck and her family of Ducklings highlights her maternal bond by placing herself in danger to protect her expansive brood. Sending her Ducklings off to the opposite bank while pretending to have a broken wing and flapping about all over the place to distract us was an apt demonstration..

A mother duck feigned a broken wing to protect her ducklings — a remarkable display of instinct & courage.

A brief sighting of a deer swimming the river way downstream was something I've only seen once previously.

9 — 005 Deer

TWEED TRAIL CHALLENGE: River Mouth to the Source

During our lunch break on an island, we had a front row seat to observe Sand Martins nesting in the riverbank opposite our vantage point. They are so fast and graceful swooping down to catch insects just above the water, followed by the spectacle of them returning to their nests. It made us wonder how they know which is theirs.

At the same time as watching the Sand Martins, we were made aware of the displeasure of a pair of Oyster Catchers as to us having had the audacity to dine on their patch. They scurried about making much noise at the opposite end of the island. We kept well clear as they obviously had a nest, and they settled as soon as we departed.

This chapter was aimed at an attempt to view the Lower Tweed Trail from an Otter's perspective, and right on cue, what should appear downstream from us but a large dog Otter. It is a truly magical sight to watch these magnificent creatures swim and dive for fish. We drifted slowly down - but once he'd clocked us, off he went.

Observing a Kingfisher is no easy task - normally they appear as just a flash of blue. This was the case when we encountered one, and sadly it was missed by various members of our party as there was no second occasion. Over the years I've been lucky enough to watch these birds in a number of instances while out fishing or walking - a magical experience.

9 — 008 Otter

9 — 010 Heron

I have a love-hate relationship with Herons due to their propensity to come and eat the fish in our garden pond. But seeing them in action, standing ramrod still while fishing at the side of the river, is a sight to behold. Also to watch them fly past with their broad wingspan and deep throated 'quaaack' is impressive.

Herons, with their broad wingspans & deep-throated calls, are as impressive in flight as they are standing motionless at the river's edge.

9 — 009 Kingfisher

Another bird we encountered was the Swift, which I'm informed is one of the fastest and most agile of avian creatures - brilliant to watch. Sitting out on the water in a canoe and looking up at these amazing birds swooping and diving at tremendous speed while catching insects proved a perfect vantage point.

Watching swifts swoop & dive at tremendous speed from the vantage point of a canoe was unforgettable.

From an Otter's perspective, I wonder what they make of (Walter) Wagtail. They must see these close up, ducking and diving while hopping from stone to stone in the shallows. As a fisherman I come across these on a regular basis and they don't appear too concerned as to my presence, and the same proved true while in a canoe.

From an otter's perspective, the darting wagtail must be a familiar companion along the river's edge.

9 — 012 Wagtail

On our journey down the river we came across a great many Swans, various of them sitting on nests which we assiduously detoured around and at a distance so as not to disturb them. But the outstanding sight was seeing these en-masse down at the river mouth, and I'm led to understand the population is much greater at different times of year.

A final detour beyond the lighthouse into the North Sea rewarded us with a pod of dolphins at play.

I have to admit at this stage to cheating in relation to the final section of our Lower Tweed journey, in that we made the decision to transfer from canoe for the last leg and instead utilise the boat trips at Paxton House and also from the Berwick Quayside. There was method in our madness, in that the latter provided the opportunity to go out beyond the lighthouse into the North Sea and watch a pod of dolphins at play - which was spectacular.

To conclude the challenge and win my wager required reporting my findings back to my dinner colleagues at the Collingwood Arms, which went as follows:

Walking the Lower Tweed takes more time than either microlight or canoe, but has advantages as well as disadvantages to the others. The view in certain circumstances is restricted, but at other times better. Access to woodland and observing four-legged wildlife while walking has benefits compared to either microlight or canoe, the same being true of access to food and drink at the various hostelries visited along the way. Also, there is the ability to engage with the towns, villages and country houses along the route - plus the opportunity to divert and explore.

The vistas from the microlight are spectacular, and provide an amazing panoramic view of the countryside as well as how the river and trail wend their way inland. The ability to see things that are totally unavailable and unknown while walking or canoeing is what makes the 'Birdseye View' such a special experience. The downside is restricted involvement with wildlife, flora and fauna, or the ability to visit interesting places along the way.

The canoe trip enables seeing all parts of the river - unlike walking the trail, where unfortunately there are parts inaccessible to us humans. The ability to engage with the birdlife and animals associated with the river is the standout aspect of utilising a canoe. The tranquil nature of this method of transport is very much a plus. The downside relates to not being in a position to engage with woodland unless disembarking from the canoe. There is also limited ability to visit the various towns, villages and country houses unless doing as previously.

To conclude: Each has their own pluses and minuses, but the combination of all three provides an amazing insight and understanding in relation to this beautiful part of the world. My recommendation - engage with them all.

TWEED TRAIL CHALLENGE 09
AN OTTER'S PERSPECTIVE

Authors & Books
Artic Convoy PQ18 – John R McKay

Thomas (Tommy) Purvis left Horncliffe School at the age of 14 to become a netsman on the River Tweed, and at 18 he became a merchant seaman involved in the infamous Artic Convoys to Russia during WW2. 'Artic Convoy PQ18' highlights the unimaginable horrors of what these entailed, and how much we owe the wartime generation. It's apt that Tommy is to feature on the Purvis family sandstone plinth at the beginning of the upper section of BAGW.

Musicians & Popular Music
Sunny Afternoon - The Kinks

A further song from the youth of Debbie and me, and appropriate as regards 'Lazing on a Sunny Afternoon' while travelling down the River Tweed in canoes with great mates - and its message in relation to putting ones troubles behind you. Spare a thought for the 'Youth of Yesterday' who made it possible for us to partake in such adventures.

Composers & Classical Music
Tutto e Bellissimo (Everything is Beautiful) – Alberto Giurioli

A composition which fits the bill in relation to completing a very special journey of discovery having walked, flown and canoed the Lower Tweed. This is a very special part of the UK, and one we highly recommend to all who are curious of the world around them and in particular those open to learning about the Borderlands.

Fine Wine
Harrow & Hope, Brut Reserve No 9, Marlow, Buckinghamshire (England)

This the final wine, and appropriate to toast what has proved an amazing and enlightening enterprise for Debbie and me as to learning not only more about the Lower Tweed and its story - but in addition, the understanding we have gained via the 'Benchmark at Grinham's Wood' initiative as to all we and others owe to an unsung and little-understood generation and their exploits which has enabled us to live the lives we do.

The Tweed – Upstream

The Tweed – Downstream

TWEED TRAIL CHALLENGE 10
BENCHMARK AT GRINHAM'S WOOD

Early on in the book, I explained the 'Origins of the Challenge' and how I came to be involved. The following taken from this:

Tweed Trail Challenge points to my inability to sit still for long, and having the boredom threshold of a gnat. Hence my engagement with a charity 'Benchmark at Grinham's Wood,' whose aims are to promote the benefits of Paths & Benches; Woodland & Wildlife; History & Commemoration; Art & Photography; and Health & Wellbeing. A small riverside community's poignant and fitting tribute to the families of past village Stalwarts who served their country during the Second World War.

What this doesn't explain is the timeline, and how the project dates back to the 16th of November 2017 when I and my fellow Trustees proposed the initial concept and registered 'Benchmark at Grinham's Wood' with the Charity Commission. At this juncture, the vision and scale of the project was smaller and restricted to the section of riverbank beyond Horncliffe to St Thomas' Island.

To cut a long and convoluted story short, a number of circumstances/situations intervened and led to the original concept of BAGW encompassing the mile of riverside path beyond Horncliffe, with the addition of the mile below to the iconic Union Chain Bridge. The COVID-19 pandemic and lockdowns created disruption to progress, but the major change related to the Tweed Forum's proposal to create a Tweed Trail from the source of the river Tweed to the mouth at Berwick-upon-Tweed.

The game-changer came about when it was thought that the lower section could well follow aspects of the existing Lower Tweed Trail and encompass the original element of Benchmark at Grinham's Wood - but also the additional downstream section to the Union Chain Bridge. A further massive boost to the project related to Robert Hunter of Horncliffe House's aim to develop a wood on his land and agreeing to this becoming Grinham's Wood. He also being the owner of a redundant fishing shiel (station) ensconced within the proposed woodland.

To those involved in a charity initiative, the message I wish to impart relates to the timescale that a project inevitably takes. As per my 50+ years in business, my mantra relates to developing a vision, then a focus as to what is to be achieved, then a strategy and business plan, followed by action plans relating to such. The final element involves driving these to a successful outcome and conclusion.

I wish to take this opportunity to thank my fellow Trustees, and all the many Friends, Volunteers, Supporters, Charitable Trusts and Funding Institutions who have made the BAGW initiative possible. All the blood, sweat and tears involved along the way has been worthwhile, and for a great cause.

So if you and others have a concept for a charity initiative - go for it, as the satisfaction to be gained from involvement and achieving your goals makes all the hard work and effort worthwhile.

This final section of the book aims to provide an insight to 'Benchmark at Grinham's Wood'. I've utilised two leaflets produced early on in the project, 'An Introduction to Our Project' and the 'Elements Involved in BAGW,' to paint a picture as to the original aims of the initiative. This is followed by an insightful speech by a fellow trustee, 'The Village They Left Behind'. Finally, a few of the Stalwart stories have been included.

The Benchmark at Grinham's Wood initiative has grown through vision, persistence & the tireless efforts of its supporters.

For further information and updates or to sign-up as a friend/supporter visit

www.bagw.co.uk

An Introduction to the Project:

'Benchmark at Grinham's Wood' is a community initiative to highlight the 'Grinham Legacy' and celebrate a Horncliffe couple who left their mark. Pierrette Grinham survived her husband Fredrick and, on her death, her French relatives generously donated the proceeds of the estate to the village.

Horncliffe subsequently benefitted from an extension and upgrade to the village hall, redevelopment of the children's play park, rejuvenation of the War Memorial, funds towards information boards relating to the restoration of the Union Chain Bridge - amongst others.

'Benchmark at Grinham's Wood' aims to recognise Fred and Pirrette, as well as the philanthropy of their French relatives via engagement with: Paths & Benches; Woodland & Wildlife; History & Commemoration; Art & Photography; and Health & Wellbeing. The initiative involves a little over two miles of river trail centred on Horncliffe, which encompasses a mile up-river, and a mile down-stream.

The 'Benchmark' and memorial bench element relates to past members of the community and their involvement (many mere teenagers at the time) in the Second World War. Each bench is dedicated to the memory of a village family, with a sandstone plinth and inset tablet recording an aspect of their wartime story for posterity.

This feeds into the element of 'History & Commemoration,' with an additional aim of highlighting that many of these individuals returned to make their living from salmon fishing via coble and net - hence the desire to commemorate what was previously - and, at that time, a vital element of the local economy.

Promotion of 'Woodland and Wildlife': The 25 acres of river bank and glen above Horncliffe, plus the 25 acres down-stream to the Union Chain Bridge, are a haven for wildlife. The memorial benches provide excellent vantage points to watch a diverse array of wildlife from the likes of salmon, otters, kingfishers, and a wide assortment of other species that frequent our river banks. A further objective involves enhancing the environment by additional tree planting across both areas of the project.

The opportunity for 'Artists & Photographers' to record spectacular scenery and wildlife is a further aim and ambition of the 'Benchmark at Grinham's Wood' initiative. The diversity of landscape, terrain and subjects provides an ideal situation for those with an artistic bent. A further wish relates to creating opportunities for those producing such works of art - to display and exhibit such.

An additional aspect of the 'Benchmark' project is promotion of 'Health & Wellbeing'. Being out in the fresh air, taking exercise and in an environment that stimulates the brain - is good for one's soul. A further facet of the initiative relates to 'A Thought for the Youth of Today & Yesterday,' in relation to those involved in the Second World War (as mere teenagers) and what they encountered during that time.

One's own troubles and issues may well pale into insignificance when related to their experiences.

The BAGW Trustees' hope and wish is that people of all ages and backgrounds are able to draw something positive from the wide array of opportunities 'Benchmark at Grinham's Wood' creates. And spare a thought for Fred, Pierrette, and the generosity of their French relatives, along with a previous inspirational generation of Horncliffe village worthies, who were all the catalysts behind this community initiative.

Artwork and sketches courtesy of Peter Knox, a Horncliffe resident and highly-respected artist.

The Elements Involved in the Benchmark at Grinham's Wood Initiative:

PHASE ONE - WOODLAND & WILDLIFE

Central to the 'Benchmark at Grinham's Wood' project is the planting of 8,000 trees on the riverside below Horncliffe to commemorate Pierrette and Fredrick Grinham (community Stalwarts for a great many years) and the generosity of their French relatives who saw fit to donate the proceeds of their estate to the village for the benefit of its inhabitants - as highlighted in 'An Introduction to Benchmark at Grinham's Wood'. The creation of the wood was deemed to be an apt and fitting tribute not only to Fred and Pierrette, but the philanthropy of the Capron Family.

A major aim of the 'Benchmark at Grinham's Wood' initiative relates to woodland and wildlife - the planting of 8,000 trees ticks this box - not only with regards to a new woodland, but in time will play its role in relation to wildlife too. The two-mile riverside path from the iconic Union Chain Bridge to St Thomas's Island above Horncliffe is a haven for wildlife, and Grinham's Wood is a welcome addition. It is a fitting tribute, but with major environmental as well as wildlife benefits - and has now become a reality.

PHASE TWO - COMMEMORATIVE BENCHES

Once again, highlighted in the introductory document to the 'Benchmark at Grinham's Wood' initiative is the desire of the local community to commemorate those village Stalwarts and their families who served their country during the Second World War. With 2025 being the 80th anniversary of the ending of the conflict, it was deemed an appropriate time to remember and honour those who made it possible for us to live our lives in freedom. It was also recognised that if their stories were not recorded now, they would be lost forever.

Work is underway to generate the funds and volunteer labour necessary to have ten memorial benches installed along the two-mile riverside path from the Union Chain Bridge to St Thomas's Island. Each bench dedicated to the memory of those from the community who served their country, and is flanked by a sandstone plinth with a tablet inset detailing elements of their wartime service and stories. The aim is to have all ten benches and plinths in situ by the Spring of 2026.

Artwork courtesy of Peter Knox, a Horncliffe resident and highly-respected artist.

PHASE THREE - FISHING SHIEL MEMORIAL

The introduction to 'Benchmark at Grinham's Wood' highlights a major aspect of employment in Horncliffe for many centuries - salmon fishing via coble and net. This once employed a great many people on the Tweed, but is now restricted to a single fishing station at the river mouth. The point being that many who returned after the War came back to the nets - a story worth recording.

Plans are underway to restore a derelict fishing shiel at Grinham's Wood as a memorial to the once-thriving salmon fishing industry on the Tweed.

Hence the intention to raise the funds necessary to re-purpose a derelict fishing shiel adjacent to Grinham's Wood and utilise this as a memorial to an ancient way of life that's now almost extinct. The plan is to stabilise the remains of the structure and build a viewing platform within. It is also to provide an interpretation panel demonstrating how the fishing station operated not so very long ago.

PHASE FOUR - FISHING COBLE MEMORIAL

Allied to the Fishing Shiel Memorial, and to highlight what this way of life once encompassed, is the restoration of a traditional fishing coble in conjunction with the renovated structure of the fishing shiel. The owners of a local business having generously donated a Tweed fishing coble, which the Trust intends to restore to its former glory and display alongside the Fishing Shiel Memorial.

PHASE FIVE - STALWARTS COPSE

The aim of phase five relates to planting a further copse of trees on land up-stream from the village. This will be on a smaller scale to that of Grinham's Wood, but is once again aimed at enhancing both the environment and wildlife habitat. The views from the memorial benches high up on the river bank are truly spectacular, and the creation of 'Stalwarts Copse' will add to this outstanding vista.

10 – Grinham's Wood

BENCHMARK AT GRINHAM'S WOOD

Prior to signing off the final manuscript for 'Tweed Trail Challenge' I made enquiries as to the initiative's progress and a précised version goes as follows: -

Phase 1 (Planting of 8,000 Trees) is now complete and achieved via grant funding from the English Forestry Commission, Tweed Forum and generous support from the Landowner (Robert Hunter).

Phase 2 (Benches & Plinths) currently underway due to grant funding approval from the Berwick-upon-Tweed Preservation Trust, Destination Tweed Community Fund and Heritage Lottery.

Phase 3 (Fishing Shiel Memorial) is about to commence due to generous support from the Catherine Cookson Foundation, the Barbour Foundation and Horncliffe's new County Councillor (Pat Lambert).

Phase 4 (Restoration of Fishing Coble) having had a 2nd boat donated has added a further dimension to the project and an area BAGW are currently looking to raise further funds to enable such.

Phase 5 (Stalwarts Copse) will proceed in the autumn when the conditions are more conducive for planting. This due to Cheviot Trees have generously agreed to donate the trees and materials.

8,000 trees planted – a milestone made possible through grants, community support & local generosity.

To learn more as to the latest status of the 'Benchmark at Grinham's Wood' initiative I recommend visiting their excellent website www.bagw.co.uk . The website also provides the ability to become a 'Friend & Supporter' being something they very much welcome and encourage.

10 — 1960's Horncliffe

TWEED TRAIL CHALLENGE 11
THE VILLAGE THEY LEFT BEHIND

The following is an insightful speech in relation to Horncliffe and given by my good friend Bill Robertson at the launch event for 'The Friends of Benchmark at Grinham's Wood'. Bill's forebears being Robertsons and Strothers, going back many generations and intertwined with village history and folklore.

It is a privilege to be able to speak about my home village, particularly in the context of this exciting project. It is also personal as Fred and Pierrette Grinham were lifelong, close friends and neighbours of my family through all the years I was growing up and after. I have fond memories of their home, in particular the parties, with Fred's lethal home brew, Pierrette's tasty food, and lots of cats. And, of course, especially fond memories of Pierrette's French nieces who summered in Horncliffe and seemed so exotic. I am still in touch with Marie-Anne, and Marie-Matilde.

But first an acknowledgement. What I have to say today is deeply indebted to Stuart Brown's invaluable research text 'Echoes that Remain'.

My intention is to provide an overview of daily life in Horncliffe. The life which for many of the conscripted men was all they knew, and which presented such a striking contrast in its simplicity and pace to what they experienced as they answered their Country's call to serve in the armed forces and go to war.

Growing up in Horncliffe, I remember Fred & Pierrette Grinham's warm hospitality.

Horncliffe was established as a defensive site as far back as pre-medieval times on a cliff overlooking a majestic curve in the river, known as a 'Horna' by Norse raiders. The embodiment of the two created the name 'Horncliffe'. Surrounding the rise on which the village was built were streams and the poorly drained land of 'the bog' and 'mad steep', where thatchers soaked their roofing materials. It was an isolated community with no through road, and it was not until the 1920s that a village sign was nailed to the first of the elm trees at the foot of the 'Coopers Brae'. Otherwise any stranger on the loop of the road from Eagle Lodge to Velvet Hall would be forgiven for bypassing Horncliffe. Before then, it stood out of sight over the crest of the hill, housing fewer than 300 inhabitants.

Of necessity it was virtually self-supporting, a tight inter-connected community. No one was without a garden for vegetables, and many kept pigs. There were two shops, a tailor, blacksmiths, joiner, a market garden, and a post office which moved constantly from one house to another as the post mistress changed. There was a farm, and the important social anchors of school, church and pub.

The architecture was not exceptional, consisting of terraces and cottages, some with thatch, some with pantiles, all fashioned from the soft pink sandstone quarried from the river bank. There were a few grander properties, Garden House, The Hollies, Cairnbank, Richmond Villa and the Avenue. The streets were unmade and partly cobbled. Electricity and mains water supply did not arrive until 1938. Before that most villagers carried their water from the 'Town Well' at the entrance to the village and from the pump in the bog field. A few houses had draw wells.

Horncliffe was a self-sufficient, close-knit community where generations of salmon fishers, market gardeners, & craftsmen lived by firmly fixed values & traditions.

Families had been salmon fishers for generations. Forgive me if I miss out some names, but Purvis, Strother, Robertson, Simpson, Cockburn, and Mole spring to mind. Of these, there were several branches and, of necessity, most were differentiated by first names. There was Big Toms, Little Toms, Big Dods and Little Dods, and, very confusingly, married women were often referred to by their maiden name.

Village life was simple. Money was scarce. But firmly fixed and observed principles and standards prevailed. Doorsteps were scrubbed, and washing was a ritual kept strictly for Mondays. It was a close-knit community, with unlocked doors. Sympathetic and supportive.

Daily life revolved around School and Church. Education was carried out in the Old School, built in 1833. Conditions had barely changed since the 19th century. Even in my day it looked like a museum of education. One large space was divided by a glazed partition to separate infants from juniors, and at age 14 they had completed their education. It would be a challenge for the diverse teaching needed for a range of abilities and ages combined with the added complication of the sons and daughters of itinerant farm workers. It would be no easy task to control many unwilling pupils, most of whom were aware that their future lay no further than the nearby river, the land or serving in a 'big house'. With no school outings or parties to relieve its monotony there was no avoiding the classroom.

Horncliffe's Old School changed little in a century.

Only once a year, and under strict supervision, did the pupils add a fourth 'R' to the 3 Rs: Remembrance, when they escaped to observe Armistice Day. They would mourn afresh the people they had never known and who had left before they were born. But the names chiselled into the stone cross before them were the names of the families they knew, and the grief of their relatives was shared and eased by the entire village. The departed were remembered. Remembrance Day would accentuate the interdependency of the community, with no real contact with the world beyond its parish.

Sundays meant Sunday School, held in the corrugated iron building set to one side of the Presbyterian church. Part of the lesson would be given inside the sparsely-decorated church, with its hard wooden pews and frosted glass windows. The remainder of the teaching was done by mothers the children all knew, singing hymns and telling Bible stories. Recompense for the hours of incarceration came with the annual picnic and the Christmas party. The trip to the seaside at Spittal was an exciting adventure beyond the bounds of the village. There was also the annual Church 'Soiree,' with secular music, ballads and recitations replacing intonations from the pulpit. The summer 'Flower Service' filled the church with posies, blessed and redistributed to the ladies of the village.

The annual Regatta and Sports Day was a long-held tradition. The course ran from the Black Hole to Under Waltham, with 'Tug of War' and Quoit competitions on the side.

Leisure activities were simple: rod fishing, snaring rabbits, collecting birds eggs, gathering frog spawn, picking wild soft fruits, exploring the fields, river banks, and the glories of the Glen and Mill. On Easter Monday, pace eggs dyed with onion skins and flowers were 'booled' on the river banks, and eaten with a picnic. In winter, out would come the sledges made by adept fathers cobbling together an ill-assorted collection of recycled wood. They were nothing like the toboggans seen in picture books. Favourite slopes were the Dummy's Hole and Cooper's Brae.

From Sunday School hymns & the Church Soirée to the annual Regatta & simple pleasures like gathering frog spawn or exploring the riverbanks, village life in Horncliffe was rooted in tradition

Childhood ended when boys became 'laddies' and followed in the footsteps of their fathers, earning their livelihood at the fisheries, some owned by their families including mine. The fishing season would begin mid-February and end mid-September. The seasons could vary in their success, depending on the nature and condition of the river. Horncliffe is at the point where the volume of water increases in a widening channel and the river slackens its pace. It is the furthest point upstream to regularly feel the effect of the North Sea tides which, when high enough, creates the conditions needed to trigger the salmon's irresistible urge to abandon sea water for fresh.

Life in Horncliffe revolved around the salmon — with men fishing through harsh seasons, families adapting to the river's rhythms, & many later serving in the war as skilled seamen & naval crew.

The lives of the fishermen were intimately connected with the life cycle and behaviour of the salmon. This impacted on families, with men sometimes living in the shiels for much of the week, fishing at night and sleeping during the day. Shiels provided basic facilities, contrasting with their tidy village homes. Work left little time for the niceties of cleaning, and any downtime was taken up with knitting and mending nets. It was a way of life developed over generations. It was a hard life, particularly at the start of the season, with snow and ice a constant threat. In spring there were floods which, while attracting fish to the river, also meant endless hours of fishing in fast-flowing muddy water to make the most of any run there might be, but without any guarantee of success.

A dispiriting task. The work was arduous and the irregular hours upset natural rhythms and ordered living, especially for the women at home who were left to deal with all the daytime activities of home and family life. Nevertheless, for the villagers, the river was their life. The urge to fish was irresistible. Even on their one free day, men were drawn to the Bank Top to study the river and assess the possibilities for the week ahead: a condition known as 'Fish Fever' or the 'Scales'.

For a few, Sunday afternoons afforded the time to take their families into a boat, bereft of nets, and bailed dry for a sail to the Chain Bridge, timing the trip to coincide with the flooding tide for an easier return.

During the hard 'close' season, no more than a few days of casual work could be expected. A tough time before the days of the dole. For those unable to rely on regular work, there was always the river to provide for badly-needed cash – poaching – not honestly earned in the eyes of the law, but perfectly acceptable in the eyes of Horncliffe.

On 3rd September 1939, life in this tight-knit, isolated village was once more disrupted by war. On that day Britain declared war on Germany, and Parliament immediately passed a wide-reaching measure. The National Service (Armed Forces) Act imposed conscription on all males aged between 18 and 41. The UK mobilised 22% of its population for military service, more than any country in the war. On the Ministry of Defence Application forms, the men of Horncliffe responded to the question about occupation as fishermen. As a result, it would appear that many men were drafted to the Royal Navy and to the ports of Hull and Grimsby. There, trawlers were converted into mine sweepers, and the gear used to trawl fish was easily adapted for mine-sweeping. The Horncliffe men, accustomed to nets, ropes and water, made ideal candidates. Others found themselves in the Merchant Navy, involved in the Atlantic and Arctic convoys, protecting essential supplies of armaments, raw materials and food. A few men found their way into the army and air force. Women were also part of the war effort. Directly in the Forces or in the Land Army, and filling gaps in the workforce. My father was in the Adriatic, tasked with clearing mines before the invasion of Italy. My mother worked for Meccano in Liverpool, which had switched production from toys to armaments.

Apart from Flight Sgt David T. Davidson RAF, all who had left returned to the village. What an extraordinary experience it must have been for this generation. They were catapulted from their tiny, close-knit community to theatres of war far from home, where they experienced different lives and cultures, an opportunity they would never otherwise have dreamt of. But they were also traumatised by the horrors of war. They shared little of their experiences. Diaries had been forbidden. Undated photographs with unidentified people and places were put away in shoe boxes in attics, leaving their war times a mystery for the post-War generation. I only learned recently about my Father's activities supporting Tito's forces against the Germans.

The men returned to a relatively unchanged village, but a knowledge of the wider world added momentum to a process of progress. Transport improved, trades died out, shops closed, new houses and schools were built. The Croft appeared at the crest of the Cooper's Brae to reveal the presence of what had been a hidden village.

Horncliffe's World War II generation was born soon after the end of the Great War in 1918. In 1920, a memorial cross was erected in front of the Church. It bears the names of the fallen. In the same year, a thatched cottage - where Oliver Cromwell took up quarters before crossing the Tweed and which had latterly been used as a social hub - was demolished. The current War Memorial Hall was erected on the empty site in 1957, the original having burned down in 1945. It is entirely fitting that some of Fred and Pierrette's generous bequest has been used to refurbish this much-loved and well utilised facility.

From close-knit rural life to the distant theatres of war, returning soldiers came home to a village forever changed.

Horncliffe's 1st & 2nd World War generations are remembered on the village memorial, a lasting tribute in the heart of the community.

These landmarks, together with Remembrance Day, will ensure that the sacrifices and achievements of the World War II generation, which gave our generation peace, will not be forgotten by the village they left behind.

THIS FAMILY IS ALL IN IT TOGETHER

Sunday Express Reporter
NEWCASTLE-ON-TYNE, Saturday.

THE "Fighting Andersons," of Causey House, Gosforth, have stepped their remarkable Service record to 100 per cent., decorations for conspicuous gallantry to five and one mention in dispatches.

HERE THEY ARE— NINE FIGHTING ANDERSONS

All nine are on active service, and not until Hitler is beaten will it be possible for them to have a reunion.

This is the family's war line-up:

1 — Colonel William Anderson, C.B., D.S.O., M.C., A.D.C. to the King, 57-year-old company director. He served throughout World War 1, and in 1931 became the first Territorial officer to command an infantry brigade in peace time. Retired from the Territorial Army in 1935 and appointed A.D.C. to the King. When World War 2 started he immediately volunteered. He has been on three years' non-stop service overseas.

2 — Mrs E. C. Anderson, his wife. When the last of the family after leaving school went straight into the Service, Mrs Anderson decided to join up, too. She became a junior commander in the A.T.S., later transferred to the F.A.N.Y.

3 — Lieutenant St. G. Anderson, D.S.C., R.N.R., elder son. Joined the Navy from school. Has been at sea in submarines for more than three years. He was recently awarded the D.S.C. for conspicuous gallantry in attacking and sinking enemy ships.

4 — Subaltern Mrs Anne Anderson, A.T.S., daughter-in-law, wife of Lieutenant St G.

5 — Lieutenant J. A. E. Anderson, M.C., the Black Watch, younger son. Enlisted as soon as he was of age and is now a veteran of the Eighth Army. Official notification was received a few days ago that he has been awarded the M.C. for conspicuous gallantry in the field. His father was awarded the same decoration for an identical act of gallantry 27 years ago.

6 — Lieut.-Commander W. D. Thorburn, R.N.V.R., son-in-

1, Father

2, Mother

3, Son

4, Son's wife

5, Son

6, Son-in-law

7, Daughter

8, Son-in-law

9, Daughter

FORBIDDEN PATHS
STUART BROWN

This, in his own words, is the remarkable true story of Stuart Brown's war — a story which began on June 12 1940 when Fusilier Stuart Brown of the Royal Northumberland Fusiliers, attached to the 51st Highland Division, was captured at St. Valery-en-Caux at the age of twenty. In one respect his war was over, but a new chapter in his life was about to open. Far removed from the heroics of Colditz, Brown was to spend most of his war on a farm in Western Poland where he was destined to fall in love, while a German prisoner, with Dora Warkentin, the beautiful young daughter of the farmer for whom he worked.

FORBIDDEN PATHS is the story of the clandestine wartime love affair of the young British soldier with the leader of the village section of the Bund Deutsche Mädchen — a liaison conducted under the constant threat of internment in a concentration camp — and their later flight together before the advance and occupation of the undisciplined and drunken Russian soldiery.

Eventually the Russian advance was to catch up with them in Danzig where they underwent some of their most terrifying experiences. At one point they had to hide together underneath a bed used for repeated and indiscriminate rape by Russian soldiers.

TWEED TRAIL CHALLENGE 12
STALWARTS STORIES

As previously explained, an important aspect of the 'Benchmark at Grinham's Wood' initiative involves research and recording the stories of Horncliffe Village Stalwarts, who served their Country during the Second World War. I was involved in compiling three of these, and would like to share my findings:

The first was Fusilier Stuart Brown, whose mother was the publican of the Fishers Arms when I was a youngster - but strangely, I had no knowledge of Stuart until a decade ago, when I came across his amazing story. The second relates to my father, Allan Herriot, who was a Captain in the 2nd Battalion 7th Gurkha Rifles - a further interesting tale. The third being my mother, Paddy Anderson/Edgar/Herriot - a WRNS (Wren) Officer in Naval Intelligence. A tragic tale, never fully divulged or shared with us, her children.

Beyond these three, much work and research by others has and is going into compiling a 'Role of Honour' and identifying those from the village who served or played their part in relation to the 1939-1945 war effort and ensuring there is a record of their involvement, and aspects of their stories are recorded for posterity.

I'm indebted to my friend Bill Robertson (his family coming from a longline of Horncliffe residents) agreeing to his masterful speech entitled 'The Village They Left Behind,' given at the launch of the BAGW initiative, and his subsequent efforts along with others in researching Horncliffe's Stalwart generation. These two pieces of work have proved invaluable to the project

To learn more as to progress visit www.bagw.co.uk and follow or add to the Stalwarts Stories.

FUSILIER STUART BROWN
4TH JUNE 1920 to 24TH MARCH 2001
7TH BATTALION ROYAL NORTHUMBERLAND FUSILIERS

Horncliffe boy Stuart Brown (whose parents were the publicans of the Fishers Arms) was eighteen years of age when he joined the local detachment of the Territorial Army in Berwick-upon-Tweed. This was after Neville Chamberlain's lamentable announcement of the 'Munich Agreement' and 'Peace in Our Time' - 30th September 1938. Less than a year later, Britain declared war on Hitler's Nazi Germany, and mobilisation of Britain's Armed Forces began in earnest.

Stuart Brown joined the Territorial Army — less than a year before Britain declared war.

Stuart's decision to sign up and depart employment as a junior reporter at the Berwick Advertiser proved unusual. The paper had just been printed and distributed when an irate PC Harry Lamb came to complain that the reporting of his impending wedding incorporated a date 48 hours in advance of the actual nuptials. Fearing the sack, or retribution from PC Lamb, he answered the TA's call for all territorials to report for duty and left a scribbled note to explain.

The consequences of his actions would prove profound on the direction of his life, of which he could have no inkling. His call-up papers provided six weeks' grace - but due to his work travails, he reported early the next morning to the TA drill hall in Berwick, and by midday was on a train to Newcastle-upon-Tyne and billeted at Gosforth race course. Subsequently he was transferred for three months to the Hampshire town of Alton to be equipped and trained for war.

Little was he to have known that it would be six long and traumatic years before he would be in a position to return home to Horncliffe. The 7th Battalion of the Royal Northumberland Fusiliers' was attached to the 51st Highland Division, and Stuart was dispatched to France on the 1st April 1940 and travelled onwards to the Saar Front of the Maginot Line with the expectation of being relieved by the French and joining the British Expeditionary Force to the North.

The battalion began to withdraw on the 20th May, with D Company (Stuart's) kept in position to cover such. By the 23rd they were back with their comrades near Etain, and in a dire position due to the collapse of the French Army. The 4th of June was Stuart's twentieth birthday, and the division launched an abortive attack on Abbeville. The subsequent days were ones of fighting and retreat, ending at St Valery and with no escape possible - they were ordered to 'lay down their arms'.

This was on the 12th of June, and the following two weeks involved a forced march of thousands of Allied troops through Belgium with little food, water or shelter. The following aspects of the journey involved open rail cars, subsequently the hold of a barge, and finally a desperate journey via enclosed cattle cars. Lack of sanitation, food and water led to lice, dysentery and worse. Eventually they arrived at a prison camp in Germany where facilities and food were scarce.

Stuart's war took him from Gosforth racecourse to France's Maginot Line, through retreat & capture, ending in a German prison camp.

Stuart and others were moved on to various camps over the following months, and eventually he ended up in Poland at Stalag XXB near Marienburg. Although the camp proved an improvement on those prior, Stuart found prison life restricting and jumped at the chance to work and live on a farm at Schonau Village looking out over the river Nogat back towards Stalag XXB. This was a move which would prove truly transformational to Stuart's life - in so many ways.

The following years involved gaining skills and experience working the land and animals - the landowner proving an enlightened individual who understood the benefits of treating his POWs in a reasonably civilised manner. But the real change related to Stuart developing an extremely dangerous and elicit romantic liaison with his daughter (Dora).

This impossible situation came to a head when the Russians smashed through the German lines and were advancing through Poland. Stuart could have left with the British POWs, but agreed to help Dora and her parents negotiate what would prove to be a truly horrendous journey. Eventually only Stuart and Dora managed to make their way through. But along the way they encountered untold horrors of mass rape and abuse - their resilience and fortitude was truly amazing.

Stuart's story of captivity culminates when they made their way through the Russian lines and into the British sector of Berlin. The story does not end there, in that getting authorisation for Dora (a German) to come to Britain proved difficult. This was finally surmounted when Stuart and Dora made it to Horncliffe and were married.

Stuart's book Forbidden Paths recounts their story, and his career - once more a journalist (News Editor and later Managing Editor of The Scotsman newspaper) - demonstrates a truly remarkable man.

CAPTAIN ALLAN DARWELL HERRIOT

23RD AUGUST 1920 TO 24TH NOVEMBER 2008
2ND BATTALION 7TH GURKHA RIFLES

When Britain declared war on Hitler's Nazi Germany on the 3rd September 1939, Allan Herriot - having just celebrated his nineteenth birthday - was studying at a Timber College in Harnosand (Sweden), after which he expected to return to the UK and join the family business of Allan Bros (Timber Merchants & Manufacturers) in Berwick-upon-Tweed. Little was he to know this would not come to pass for six long years, and with no concept as to what lay ahead.

In 1939, Allan Herriot's plans for a timber career were replaced by six years of wartime service, beginning with a dramatic escape from Sweden.

Herriot folklore has it that Allan had an interesting and testing time (due to Hitler's Nazi blitzkrieg in Europe) getting passage to the UK - a journey which involved a flight to Rotterdam and then an unofficial sailing to London. On his return, he was horrified to find his physical grading rated as 3 (due to poor eyesight), and he was posted to the Army Pay Corp in Leeds. For someone who excelled at rugby, cricket, boxing and swimming, this was a devastating blow and required a solution.

Attempts to join the RAF failed, but subsequently he discovered that he was eligible to join the Indian Army as a lowly Officer Cadet. He duly applied and was accepted, and was soon aboard the SS Maloja sailing from Greenock, destination Durban and onward to Bombay, then via train to Bangalore and Officer Training Camp. He was subsequently commissioned into the 7th Gurkha Rifles and transferred to their Regimental Centre at Palampur in the Himalayas, north of Lahore.

He was posted to North Africa in 1943 to Camp No.8 besides the Mena Pyramids and Sphinx, then subsequently to 2nd Battalion 7th Gurkha Rifles in Lebanon (inland from Tripoli). This involved training as mountaineer, snow and ski troops. Thereafter they were under notice to invade the Greek Island of Kos. However, an attack on Leros failed, and the advance on Kos was cancelled. Next he moved north to the Turkish frontier, followed by a period in Palestine. Then onwards to the Bitter Lakes (Suez Canal) to train for opposed landings. He then embarked for destination unknown, which proved to be Taranto at the Heel of Italy.

From the Pyramids of Egypt to the mountains of Lebanon & the shores of Italy, his wartime journey spanned continents & campaigns.

12 - Allan Herriot Pay Corp 1939

Allan, at this stage a Captain with the 2nd Battalion 7th Gurkha Rifles (part of the 4th Indian Division), went into battle at Cassino. Allied casualties were a staggering 55,000 in this epic four month struggle to take the Monastery at Monte Cassino. As a battalion intelligence officer on Point 593 overlooking the Monastery, he latterly admitted to suffering recurring nightmares throughout the remainder of his life with reference to what he encountered.

Having been withdrawn from Cassino, the 7th Gurkha Rifles' next port of call was on the Adriatic above Luanciano, opposite Orsga and Ortona. Allan recalled being in a forward observation post for stints of three days at a time, with only carrier pigeons for communication. They followed up the Adriatic coast, (in his words) mopping up German resistance.

He records a 24 hour stopover at Assisi and seeing the magnificent tomb of St Francis (war damaged), and also coming down from the hills to Perugia which he entered as a one-man patrol to establish if the enemy had departed. Luckily it was unoccupied. Subsequently he recounts rest and recuperation in Rome, which led to unintended consequences.

After this, his memoir states it was off to Arezzo, up the River Arno from Florence and the site of increasingly serious fighting. Once again, he reports being sent forward to see if the town was occupied by the Germans - but it was not. The next stage involved crossing over the mountains to the Adriatic front and the enemy's major defensive positions on the Gothic Line.

As a Captain with the 7th Gurkha Rifles, Allan fought through Monte Cassino & along Italy's Adriatic coast, enduring some of the fiercest battles of the war.

Following this was assignment to Gubbio, which he describes as one of those fascinating historical walled towns. The enemy were said to have withdrawn - Allan was dispatched in a jeep with three riflemen to confirm - but once again the enemy had departed.

The following action led to a 'Battle Honour,' where a combined Gurkha force of the 2nd Bn 7th GR, 1st Bn 9th GR and 1st Bn 7th GR broke through the Gothic Line at Tavoletto. Then onwards to San Marino, which was taken unopposed. Allan's last operation in Italy involved the defended valley beyond, which he describes as not being particularly successful. The jeep he was travelling in overturned, and his commanding officer had to be invalided out - which, in Allan's words, left an inadequate second in command. Their night time attack was repulsed with heavy casualties.

12 — Allan Herriot Gurkha 1940

They were then relieved by another battalion, with their next move via the southern port of Bari to Greece. This was where Allan's escapade in Rome, involving a lost truck and a threated court martial, led to his fellow officers having him (swiftly) sent ahead to Greece, commanding the advance party. The court martial never came about.

Their vessel, a Landing Craft Tank (LCT), took them to Preveza, a small fishing village with an enormous Turkish castle in which they were billed. A peaceful and pleasant time was disrupted when comrades in Missalongi (Gulf of Corinth) were attacked by ELAS partisans, leaving them exposed. Hence they were withdrawn to Patras and Brigade HQ.

Allan's final stint in Greece was to Kilkis, up country towards the SW Bulgarian border in mid-summer, and he mentions Greek country dancing every Saturday night in the village square - which they joined in. Subsequently he went on leave to Berwick for the first time since heading out to India. Leave over, he re-joined his battalion back in Palampur (India) at their regimental centre, to train and prepare for what was thought to be a landing on Japan.

Allan's war and interaction with his beloved Gurkhas left a lasting effect. He possessed an incredible karma and approach to life which came from his many and varied experiences gained while serving his Country.

12- Allan Herriot 1944

Allan's service took him from Rome to Greece, where time in Preveza's fishing village ended abruptly with partisan attacks. In 1945, he fought against ELAS forces near Patras before moving on to Salonica, briefly serving as Acting Adjutant.

Spring 1945 saw Allan's 7th Gurkhas involved in action inland from Patras against the ELAS partisans (communists). He records removing ELAS from the valley and village of Claus, and consuming excellent regional wines. Then onwards to Salonica, where he briefly became Acting Adjutant while a colleague went home on leave to the UK.

This never came about due to the atomic bombs being dropped on Hiroshima and Nagasaki (August 6th 1945), and the war subsequently coming to an end. Allan's abiding belief is that this saved his life. Prior to being demobbed and going home, he was involved for a short while in preparations relating to the 'Partition of India,' which he found shameful.

To learn more, a book (now out of print) found in Allan's possessions after his death - 'The Monastery' by F. Majdalany - provides an insight into what he and others encountered at the battle of Monte Cassino. A further book being 'Monte Cassino' by Mathew Parker. Also a recent work by James Holland, 'Cassino 44,' helps to explain the epic struggle involved in the taking of the Monastery at Cassino.

WRNS OFFICER
PATIENCE DOROTHY VERTY ANDERSON/EDGAR/HERRIOT

4TH SEPTEMBER 1920 TO 13TH OCTOBER 1995
WOMEN'S ROYAL NAVAL SERVICE

Patience Dorothy Verty Anderson was, from a young age, known to all as Paddy. With a line-up of such names, it's not difficult to see how this came to be. The reference as to the surnames of Anderson, Edgar and Herriot requires further explanation - which will be revealed as Paddy's story unfolds. Her children knew very little as to her wartime story other than her being a Wren Officer: Having signed the 'Official Secrets Act,' any question asked in relation to such was batted away by the threat of immense consequences if she was to reveal such. Typical of that wartime generation.

But with hindsight, the trauma and loss she endured may well explain more as to why this topic was never addressed.

Prior to the Second World War, Paddy spent time in Germany as a nanny for a family's young children and saw first-hand via incidents such as Kristallnacht (the suppression of the Jews) during Adolf Hitler and his abhorrent Nazi regime's rise to power. This may well be the reason why she signed up to become an Officer in the newly formed Women's Royal Naval Service. But her family's illustrious military background may well have had some influence upon the decision.

A newspaper article in The Sunday Express, 5th December 1943, provides an insight to Paddy and her family's military credentials - 'The Fighting Andersons' of Causey House, Gosforth, Newcastle-upon-Tyne:

Father Colonel William Anderson CB. DSO. MC. ADC to the King. Mother Gladys originally a junior Commander in the A.T.S. later transferred to F.A.N.Y. Older brother Lieutenant St George Anderson DSC - Royal Navy serving aboard Submarines. Sister-in-law Anne Anderson in the ATS. Younger brother Lieutenant James Aidan Robb Anderson MC - Army (Black Watch). Older sister Elizabeth Anderson originally a Sergeant in the A.T.S transferred to F.A.N.Y. Brother-in-law Lieutenant Commander Douglas Thorburn - Royal Navy serving aboard the Battleship Valiant. Lieutenant Jack Edgar (Paddy's husband) - Royal Navy serving aboard Submarines. Finally Paddy, an officer in the W.R.N.S.

Patience 'Paddy' Anderson, bound by the Official Secrets Act, rarely spoke of her service as a Wren Officer. Inspired by time in Germany & her families military credentials she joined the Women's Royal Naval Service.

It should be noted that Paddy's brothers both made their mark while serving their Country: St George a submarine Commander and highly decorated, Robb a Major in the Black Watch - another much-decorated individual.

From what little the family have been able to glean, Paddy spent much of her service life at Rosyth and Donibristle in the Firth of Forth (Scotland). One tale she told related to meeting Princess Marina of Kent when she was visiting Rosyth as Commandant of the W.R.N.S. The Lady obviously made a great impression on Paddy and her colleagues, as this tale was recounted to me many years later. The visit is well document in the Royal Archives at Windsor Castle, and provides a fascinating insight to the life of a Wren and the vital role they played in 'Freeing Men for the Fleet'.

Paddy Anderson, from a distinguished military family served as a Wren Officer at Newcastle, Rosyth & Donibristle, famously meeting Princess Marina of Kent during her wartime service.

Paddy married a dashing young Naval Officer Jack Edgar of Callerton Hall (Northumberland) on the 11th April 1942. Jack at that time was serving aboard HM Submarine Thunderbolt. The vessel had a tragic start, in that originally it was called the 'Thetis' and on sea trials off Liverpool Bay failed to resurface with the shocking loss of 100 lives. The vessel was later salvaged and refitted to become Thunderbolt, and served successfully in various theatres of war.

In April 1942, Paddy married Naval Officer Jack Edgar, who served aboard the salvaged submarine Thunderbolt.

This is where tragedy unfolds in that Paddy, as a Wren Officer involved in intelligence gathering, became aware Thunderbolt was overdue, out of contact and possibly lost. The submarine had just left Malta on her seventh full Mediterranean patrol, and on the night of March 12/13th 1944 encountered an enemy convoy and torpedoed the freighter Esterel - leading to catastrophic consequences for Thunderbolt. The submarine was subsequently harried for the next 24/30 hours by the sloop Cicogna, commanded by Capitano di Corvetta Augusto Migliorini - an ex-submariner. A game of cat and mouse ensued, culminating in the destruction of Thunderbolt.

HMS Thunderbolt was sunk after a deadly pursuit by the Italian navy.

The sting in the tale was that Paddy's family have a letter from the Admiralty informing her Thunderbolt was missing - but as the Germans and Italians were thought to be unaware, she would have to remain silent. For someone just short of her second wedding anniversary, one can only imagine the turmoil and anguish this must have wrought. It would be many years later before Paddy would learn what actually took place on that fateful day in March 1944.

THIS FAMILY IS ALL IN IT TOGETHER

Sunday Express Reporter
NEWCASTLE-ON-TYNE, Saturday.

THE "Fighting Andersons," of Causey House, Gosforth, have stepped their remarkable Service record to 100 per cent., decorations for conspicuous gallantry to five and one mention in dispatches.

HERE THEY ARE— NINE FIGHTING ANDERSONS

1, Father   2, Mother

3, Son   4, Son's wife

5, Son   6, Son-in-law

7, Daughter   8, Son-in-law   9, Daughter

All nine are on active service, and not until Hitler is beaten will it be possible for them to have a reunion.

This is the family's war line-up:

1—Colonel William Anderson, C.B., D.S.O., M.C., A.D.C. to the King, 57-year-old company director. He served throughout World War 1, and in 1931 became the first Territorial officer to command an infantry brigade in peace time. Retired from the Territorial Army in 1935 and appointed A.D.C. to the King. When World War 2 started he immediately volunteered. He has been on three years' non-stop service overseas.

2—Mrs E. C. Anderson, his wife. When the last of the family after leaving school went straight into the Service, Mrs Anderson decided to join up, too. She became a junior commander in the A.T.S., later transferred to the F.A.N.Y.

3—Lieutenant St. G. Anderson, D.S.C., R.N.R., elder son. Joined the Navy from school. Has been at sea in submarines for more than three years. He was recently awarded the D.S.C. for conspicuous gallantry in attacking and sinking enemy ships.

4—Subaltern Mrs Anne Anderson, A.T.S., daughter-in-law, wife of Lieutenant St G.

5—Lieutenant J. A. R. Anderson, M.C., the Black Watch, younger son. Enlisted as soon as he was of age, and is now a veteran of the Eighth Army. Official notification was received a few days ago that he has been awarded the M.C. for conspicuous gallantry in the field. His father was awarded the same decoration for an identical act of gallantry 27 years ago.

6—Lieut.-Commander W. D. Thorburn, R.N.V.R., son-in-law. Has been at sea since the start of the war and taken part in several important actions. He and his two brothers-in-law have taken part in the same naval engagement.

7—Mrs M. E. Thorburn, daughter, was a sergeant in the A.T.S., transferred to F.A.N.Y. and is serving in the same unit as her mother.

8—Lieutenant J. O. Edgar, R.N., son-in-law. Served in the famous submarine Thunderbolt. Is still in submarines. Has been mentioned in dispatches for gallantry while attacking enemy convoys.

9—Third Officer P. D. V. Edgar, W.R.N.S., daughter. Although the youngest of the family, she is senior in rank to her mother.

Restaurant car is canteen for rail workers

Evacuated L.N.E.R. office workers have a mobile canteen in a restaurant car parked on a siding in East Anglia and centrally heated by steam from a railway engine.

All the cooking is done in a converted kitchen car.

An official of the company said yesterday that where offices have been evacuated to country districts restaurant cars have solved the problem of accommodation and food. About half a dozen are used for this purpose.

12 - HM Submarine Thunderbolt

12 - Allan & Paddy (Later in Life)

Having recounted her tale one can only have sympathy & respect for all she had endured and achieved.

As her son, when compiling Paddy's story I came across a book - The Admiralty Regrets by CET Warren & James Benson - which recounts the story of the 'Thetis' and 'Thunderbolt'. The book had been Mum's personal copy, of which up to that point I had no prior knowledge. A special moment was finding she'd secreted a photograph of Jack inside the jacket cover. The book wasn't published until 1958, and it recounts the story of Thunderbolt's final hours.

My mother was 38 and I was 6. To learn the lurid final details of Thunderbolt's demise 14 years after she had lost her husband must have been traumatic. But the point I would like to emphasise is that she never shared this with any of the family - it was a taboo subject. She was an amazing lady who spent her life helping others. Mum had her demons, but having recounted her tale one can only have sympathy and respect for all she had endured and achieved.

My final word relates to Paddy (my mum) marrying Allan Herriot (my Dad) in 1948 - his being the prior Stalwart's story. My father in his memoir relates, 'We grew together slowly' - but he also recounted: 'Over time she grew to love me.' He worshipped the ground she walked on - and I am pleased to report they led a good life together.

HORNCLIFFE STALWARTS ROLL OF HONOUR

In relation to the Benchmark at Grinham's Wood Charitable Trust's intention to produce a Roll of Honour featured on a sandstone plinth alongside their Fishing Shiel Memorial recording all the Stalwarts from the village who answered their Country's call to serve in the Second World War (1939-45). At the stage I had to present the final manuscript to Extremis (my publishers): The BAGW Trustees along with various Friends & Supporters were planning a further event in Horncliffe village hall to update the community as to progress, but also as 'A Fishing Expedition to Gather Information on Horncliffe's Stalwarts'. Their aim and intention to ensure the record can be as accurate and complete as possible and engage with as many of the Stalwarts' relatives and associates as possible.

Horncliffe's Roll of Honour seeks to record every Stalwart.

I had originally hoped to include the Roll of Honour in my book – but this will now have to wait and be revealed at the launch of the Fishing Shiel Memorial.

I have the utmost admiration for how Horncliffe's wartime generation returned to live with dignity & resilience, proving an inspiration despite their unimaginable experiences.

I thought it worth adding: Having grown up in Horncliffe, I was blissfully unaware so many from our small community had been in the forces. Their wartime experiences were not something that was shared, which leads me to believe the horrors as to what they had seen or done was not to be divulged with the likes of us who had not been involved. I have the utmost admiration as to how they returned to life in Horncliffe and proved an inspirational example to us, the post-war generation, in relation to how they got on with life despite their unimaginable experiences. Hence I salute them all, and delighted they are now to be recognised and honoured for the part they played.

To learn more as to progress visit www.bagw.co.uk and follow or add to the Stalwarts' Stories.

Z COMPANY, 9TH BATTALION ROYAL NORTHUMBERLAND FUSILIERS

This particular aspect of 'Tweed Trail Challenge' relates to Norham (the neighbouring village) as much as Horncliffe, and has come about due to material gained from a booklet 'Norham: A Place to Remember' - as well as information provided by a Grandfather to his Grandson for a GCSE exam assignment (35 years ago). These stories have led to an additional Phase being added to the Benchmark at Grinham's Wood initiative. This to be a further poignant and unusual memorial with the intention of finding a suitable location which will do justice to what is an amazing story. The following two related pieces help explain as to how and why this has come about.

12 - Z Company

Extract from 'Norham: A Place to Remember':

Those young men from the village (Norham) who had joined the Territorial Army were part of 'Z' Company, 9th Battalion Royal Northumberland Fusiliers, landing in France a month before the German Blitzkrieg in May 1940, at which time Robert Guthrie and Alexander Hettle were taken prisoner. The Fusiliers were evacuated from Dunkirk shortly afterwards. Following a period of reforming and intense training the men embarked on the three month journey to the Far East, arriving in early February 1942. As the ships approached Singapore they came under Japanese air attack with the Battalion suffering its first casualties. The men spent the next nine days defending Singapore against the Japanese. When the surrender came on 15th February they awaited their fate, which was to be prisoners of war for more than three years, suffering harsh treatment and deprivation at the hands of their Japanese and Korean guards. They were then taken to work on the infamous Burma-Siam Railway where some of them died of dysentery because of the conditions they endured in the camps and the treatment meted out by their captors. The use of the atomic bomb on Japanese cities hastened the surrender in August 1945. Those men who survived returned home in the autumn, to be haunted by their experiences for the rest of their lives.

Extract from a GCSE exam assignment (1990):

This story coming about and only made possible via Mark Straughen a Norham resident and the Grandson of George Straughen (as featured in the picture of 'Z' Company from 'Norham a Place to Remember'). 35 years ago Mark made the insightful and significant decision to make the subject of his GCSE English exam assignment about his Grandfather George's extraordinary war time service and unimaginable travails. Having interviewed his Grandfather and discussed the subject at great length, Mark learnt of a truly remarkable story which helped save British and Allied Servicemen from death or captivity at the hands of the Germans on the beaches of Dunkirk in 1939: Hence one which deserves to be shared, as well as celebrated.

My Grandfather and his comrades from the 9th Battalion Royal Northumberland Fusiliers sailed to Cherbourg from Southampton on April 23rd 1940 – St Georges Day (the patron saint of their regiment). From Cherbourg the men moved to the small town of MonChebretton where they stayed under canvas. They had only been there a few days when the Germans pushed down through Belgium into France (hence bypassing the Maginot Line). For the first time the troops encountered a new type of warfare – Blitzkrieg – where small areas were totally destroyed by dive-bombing planes, followed by tanks and finally infantry.

The 9th Battalion were sent to a small village called Steinbeck, where they suffered heavy casualties including their Company Commander. From here the troops started to retreat back to Dunkirk. During the withdrawal, one of George's friends from the village (Alec Hettle) was on duty in a machine-gun post on the top of a ridge with two other fusiliers. The soldier on his right was suddenly struck down by a piece of shrapnel, from a mortar blast, which sliced through his helmet and killed him instantly. On seeing this Alec got such a shock that he fainted and was totally unconscious. The other soldier turned round and thought both men were dead, so left them. Hours later Alec woke up and walked in the direction of his own lines only to find that the whole area was under German control. He was subsequently taken prisoner and remained so until the end of the war in 1945.

The remainder of the troops had now reached Dunkirk or that area (George was actually at Neuwport 15 miles North of Dunkirk) and joined the massive queues for the evacuation boats. The Fusiliers formed a cordon around the beach, George's Company was under the command of a young Corporal, this man was so scared of the shells landing that he began to cry and was about to desert his post, when one of the soldiers put a rifle to his head and said "If you move I'll shoot your bloody head off". Without a leader and discipline the whole company could have been wiped out.

Unfortunately the water was extremely shallow so no ships could get close to the beach, so small rowing boats with two or three sailors were sent to pick up the troops and take them back to the ships. This was a slow process as each boat could only take six men per trip. All the time the soldiers were on the beach they were constantly being attacked by 'Stuka' dive-bombers with their infamous scream as they plummeted towards earth prior to dropping their bombs.

George and his comrades could have waited for hours, if not days, but for a large stroke of luck. The sea was not only rough, but the Luftwaffe pilots had recognised by dropping bombs into the water they were destroying as well as capsizing the small boats and stopping their rescue missions. The Company Sergeant Major approached George and five of the other Norham and Horncliffe men and said he wanted volunteers to swim out and attempt to re-float a boat. He picked them because they were all Tweed-siders and knew about craft of this size due to their up-bring and involvement with salmon fishing. In no time they had the boat righted – the secret being to turn this over from the stern, end to end, not on its side which only fills them with water. Having re-floated the boat and demonstrated the technique to others were then able to row out to a rescue ship.

Memorial to Local Nets-Men and their Exploits at Dunkirk:

Having recently had a further fishing coble donated, the Benchmark at Grinham's Wood Trustees intend for this to become a fitting memorial to the heroism and skill of George Straughan (Snr) and his fellow compatriots of 'Z' Company in conjunction with other River Tweed nets-men and to celebrate their exploits at Dunkirk. The objective is to utilise a coble in an upturned manner with a series of Silhouette Tommy's looking on and provide an information plaque recording their remarkable tale.

If you would like to help and contribute to this worthwhile charitable initiative and ensure this further memorial aspect becomes a reality please visit www.bagw.co.uk to donate or become a Friend & Supporter of Benchmark at Grinham's Wood.

For those visiting our beautiful part of the World and engaging with Tweed Trail Challenge I recommend visiting the 'Admiral Ramsey Museum' situated a dozen or so miles from Horncliffe, on the outskirts of Leitholm. Admiral Sir Bertram Ramsay was the Mastermind and organiser of the evacuation of Dunkirk and the man to whom George Straughen, 'Z' Company, and 300,000+ other souls owe so much. The museum does an excellent job in recording his amazing exploits and achievements.

TWEED TRAIL CHALLENGE 12 STALWARTS STORIES

One last book:
The Forgotten Highlander – Alistair Urquhart

This a book I came across when reading the obituary of this amazing man and his story (and apt in relation to the men of 'Z' Company and their time as Japanese POW's). Alistair served in Singapore prior to the Japanese invasion, subsequently incarcerated in the notorious Changi Jail, followed by forced labour on the Death Railway, later sunk on a Hell Ship to Japan, then a slave labourer in a coal mine on the Japanese mainland and a witness to the atomic bomb being dropped on Nagasaki.

One last song:
We'll Meet Again – Vera Lynn

While checking the final manuscript, graphics and layout for 'Tweed Trail Challenge' I happened to be in East Sussex with Debbie looking after our two youngest Grandchildren (Sandy & Rory). While there we visited the Newhaven Fort which possess some amazing exhibits relating to its history and in particular the 1st & 2nd World Wars. One such exhibit told the story of Dame Vera Lynn the 'Forces Sweetheart' – hence the late decision to add her iconic war time song 'We'll Meet Again'.

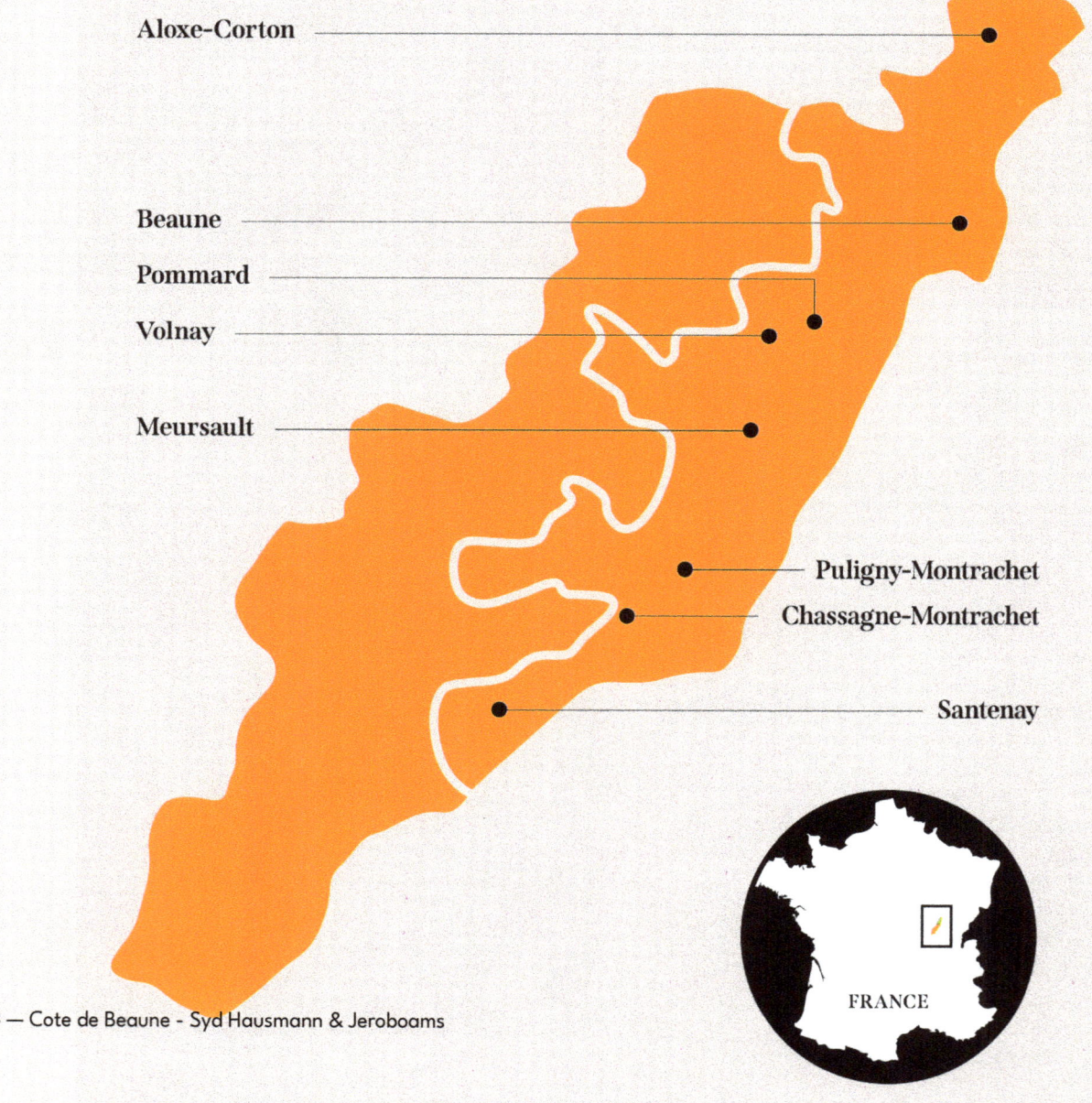

TWEED TRAIL CHALLENGE 13
LOVE LETTER TO BURGUNDY

The wines encountered within 'Tweed Trail Challenge' make out that Debbie and I are knowledgeable wine connoisseurs. Truth be told, this accolade relates to our son Simon, whose passion is wine - aptly demonstrated by the following piece he put together for Jeroboam's (Si heads up their fine wine team in London). This is also an opportunity to thank him in relation to his help and advice regards all the broad assortment of wines enjoyed on our adventure.

LOVE LETTER TO BURGUNDY

Love Letter to Burgundy

Working in the wine trade, one is often asked the question by those with a more casual relationship with grapes: "So, what is your favourite wine region"? My reply is quick and never wavers. "Simple. The region that changed and shaped my life. Burgundy".

It was March 2004. As a fresh faced 18-year-old (temporary) university dropout, I was, unknowingly, about to embark on a vinous voyage that would not only go on to define my love of this hallowed wine region, but also change my life forever.

I arrived at the Holbeck Ghyll Country House Hotel, then one of the finest small luxury hotels in the Lake District, eager to learn about restaurants and fine dining. Nine months later, I left as a Junior Sommelier with a passion for the finest Burgundy, having been paid to navigate one of the most underrated Côte d'Or-focused wine lists in the country at the time.

It was not all plain sailing; Burgundy is a complex mistress, after all. On one of my first days, I distinctly remember serving a discerning couple who pointed to and ordered a bottle of 1999 Domaine Roulot, Meursault Les Meix Chavaux. Lacking in knowledge and decent French, I butchered the pronunciation of "Roulot", "Meursault" and "Les Meix Chavaux"! They obviously saw something in my youthful ignorance, as they gave me a glass to taste. I can still remember the clarity, definition, energy, concentration and length of that wine. It was like nothing I had tasted before: all citrus peel, pear and white flowers, wrapped around tongue-tingling minerality. Obviously, at the time, I could not describe these sensations, but what I did know was that this was the region for me, and I wanted more!

When not running the gauntlet of a Michelin-starred service, I would be found with a copy of The World Atlas of Wine by my side. From there, I begin to decipher the difference between Chablis and Chassagne, Gevery and Givry, Montrachet and Macon, Volnay and Vosne. I was helped on this journey of study by having access to such producers as Domaine Raveneau, Coche-Dury, Roumier, Rousseau, Denis Mortet, Lamy and many more. I must add, all of which were much more affordable to the mere mortal back then!

Fast forward twenty years, and I now find myself a veteran of over 15 years in the wine trade, many of those having been spent working for some of the most recognisable names in the world of wine. This industry has not only offered me a job which I am passionate about, but it has also given me the opportunity to visit and explore, on numerous occasions, the region which defines my love of wine and for which everything else is compared to: Burgundy.

It was like nothing I had tasted before: all citrus peel, pear & white flowers, wrapped around tongue-tingling minerality. I knew this was the region for me, and I wanted more.

Burgundy brings you closer together through shared experiences... whatever the highs or lows, it is a region you will never forget. It is both a constant and yet leaves you wanting more.

But what is it that makes Burgundy so romantic and special to me, and many others around the world? Is it the wines themselves? The terroir? The winemakers? The history and heritage? The beautiful surroundings? Or the people you drink it with? Once again, the answer is simple. It is all of the above. Great wine is best shared in great company, and with those who appreciate what you are consuming. I have been fortunate enough to drink some of the finest, most memorable and valuable bottles of wine with people who I am lucky to call my friends. I have visited cellars with them, tasted with winemakers, and walked through extraordinary vineyards. Burgundy brings you closer together through shared experiences, whether that is the monumental highs of sipping perfect bottles of 2002 Corton Charlemagne from Domaine Coche-Dury, 1990 Rousseau Chambertin and 2004 Montrachet from Ramonet, or encountering the earth-shattering disappointment of opening a faulty bottle of 1992 Domaine Leflaive Batard or a corked magnum of 2009 Dujac Clos Saint-Deni. Whatever the highs or lows, Burgundy is a region that you will never forget. It is both a constant and yet leaves you wanting more, it becomes part of the wine lover that you are.

*Cheers to discovery.
Cheers to vinous pleasure at whatever the cost.*

Cheers to Burgundy.

WILDLIFE PHOTOGRAPHER
RONNIE HEK

Ronnie is one of those people who has grasped life and has a wide array of talents: Singer Songwriter, Raconteur, Tartan Designer, Metal Detectorist and an accomplished and passionate Wildlife Photographer, aptly demonstrated via the amazing imagery incorporated within 'Tweed Trail Challenge'. I don't profess to have the skill or patience that is necessary to capture birds, animals and fish in the wild. Ronnie possesses such talents in spades, as captured in the amazing assortment of wildlife images within the book. Ronnie's input to 'Tweed Trail Challenge' has been truly transformational and of immense value. To learn and see more of Ronnie's work follow him on Facebook and Instagram, or visit his exhibition at the Chainbridge Honey Farm (Horncliffe) as featured in Chapter 3 – Paxton to Horncliffe.

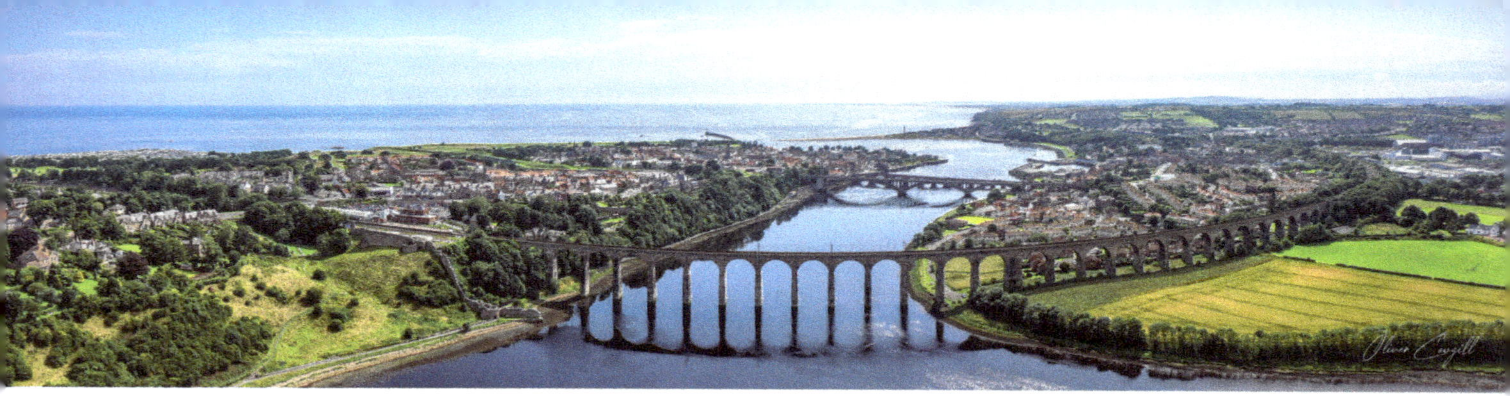

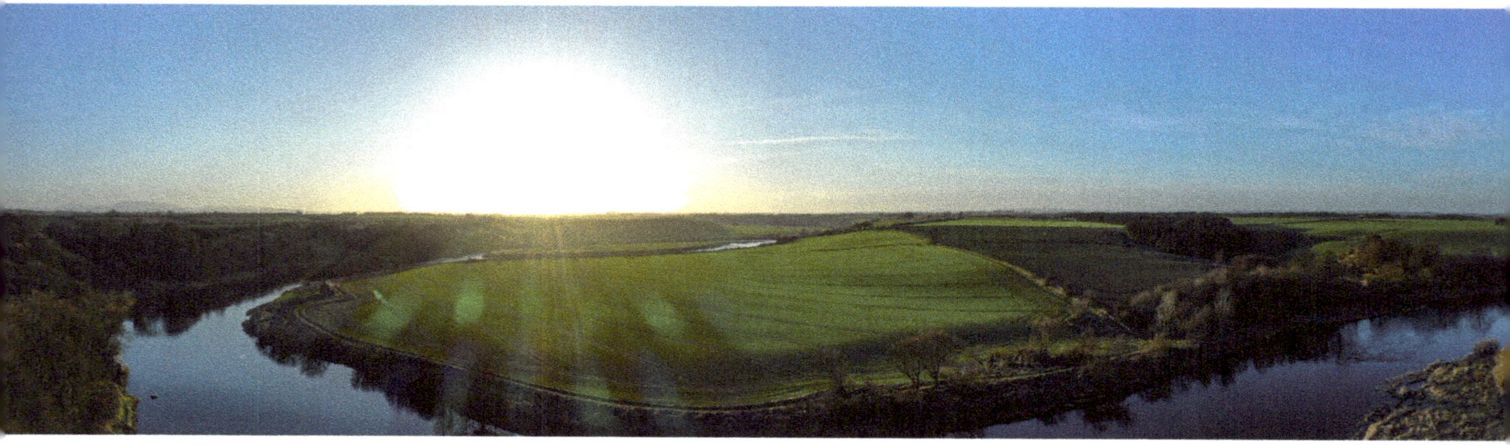

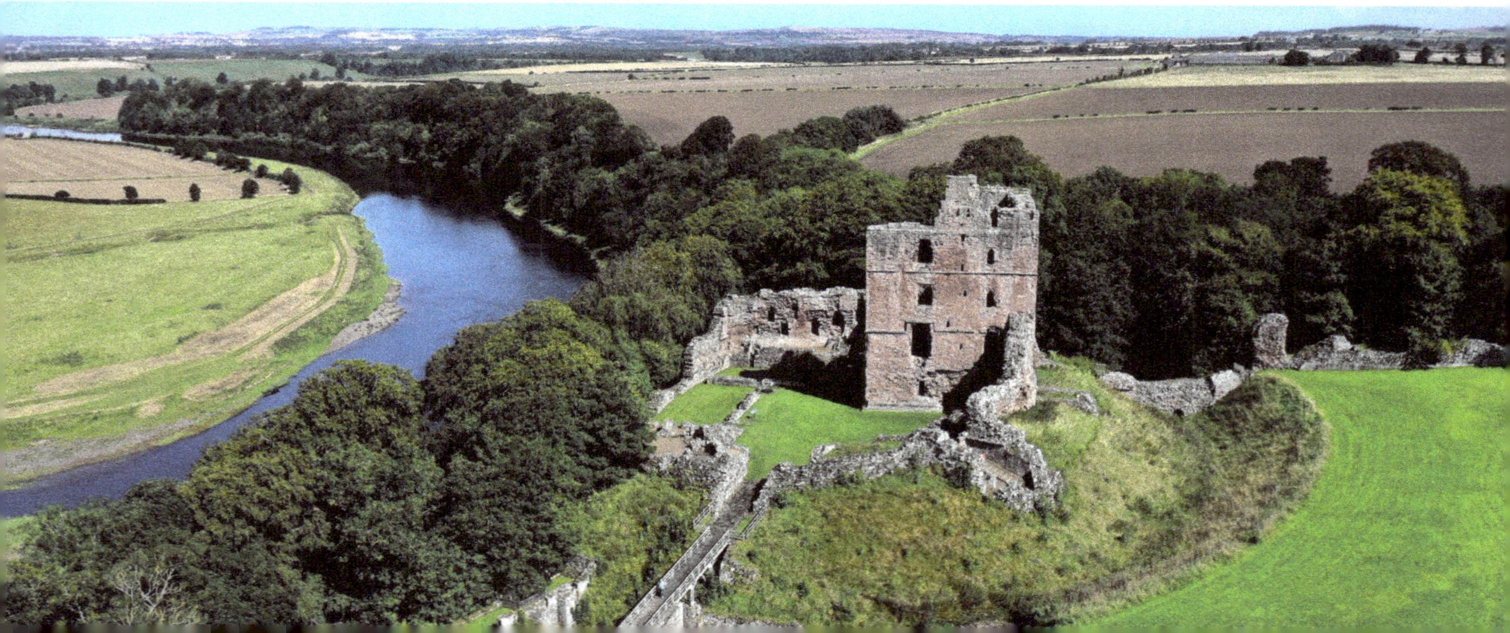

DRONE PILOT PHOTOGRAPHER
OLLIE COWGILL

Ollie is a Horncliffe resident and a wizard in the world of Tech which has long since developed into becoming a Master Drone Pilot & Photographer. As can be assessed from the drone imagery incorporated into 'Tweed Trail Challenge' (all courtesy of Mr Ollie Cowgill) he is truly a maestro and I cannot thank him enough for all his help, input, effort and support in the development and creation of the book. I am a keen amateur photographer - but add in the complexity of a drone, something totally outside my comfort zone and ability. So Ollie: A massive thank you, the book would be the poorer without your involvement. To learn more follow him on social media @Ollie_Cowgill

PHOTOGRAPHY CREDITS

A big thank you to the following who helped resolve a number of photographic issues which arose.

Michael Barron FRPS – Michael's image of the Royal Border Bridge (illuminated) got me out of a hole as the lights were not functioning correctly when attempting to photograph this.

Walter Baxter – Photographing the Border Belle while on-board proved a failure hence the skipper organised and arranged permission to utilise Walter's brilliant image of the boat and bridge.

Jim Gibson Photographer – My attempts to photograph the fishermen at the mouth of the Tweed were not up to scratch, along with my image of the Picture Gallery at Paxton House - Jim coming to my rescue.

Paul Herron – The Robson Family (Proprietors of the Honey Farm) came to my assistance in relation to an image of the humble honey bee and wished to ensure I credited Paul for his handiwork.

Stephen Whitehorne Photography – I was looking for 2 seasonal images of the Hirsel Estate and having seen Stephen's on-site photographic exhibition, he was kind enough to provide such.

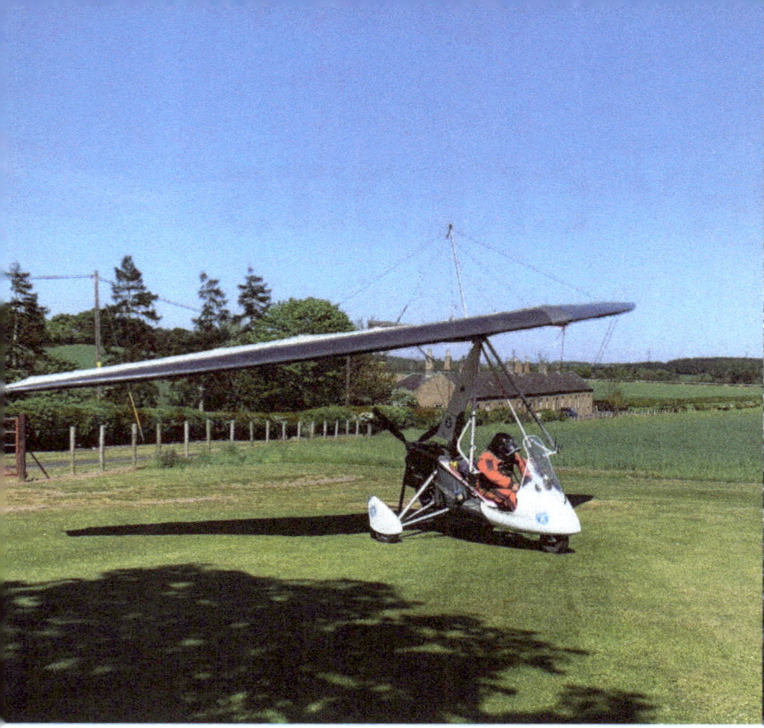
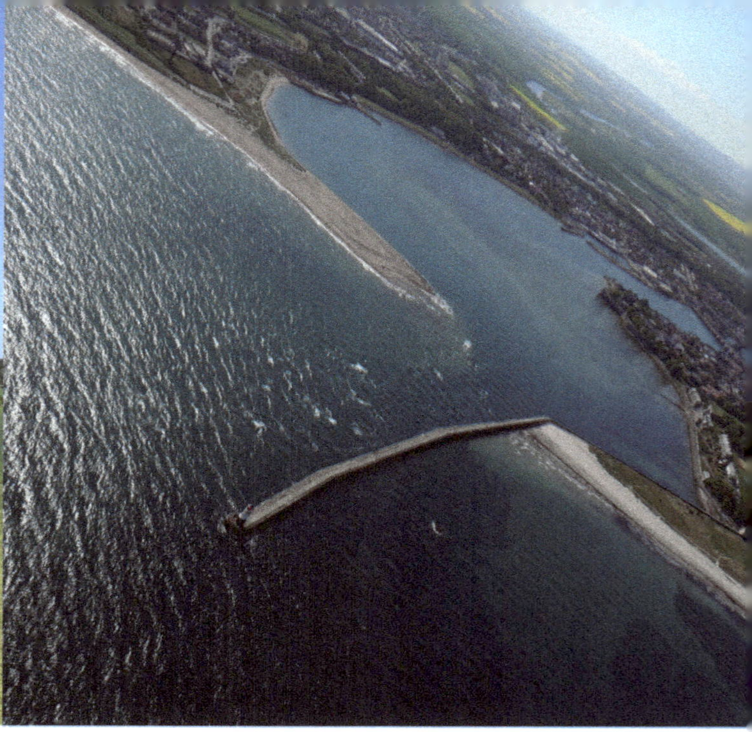
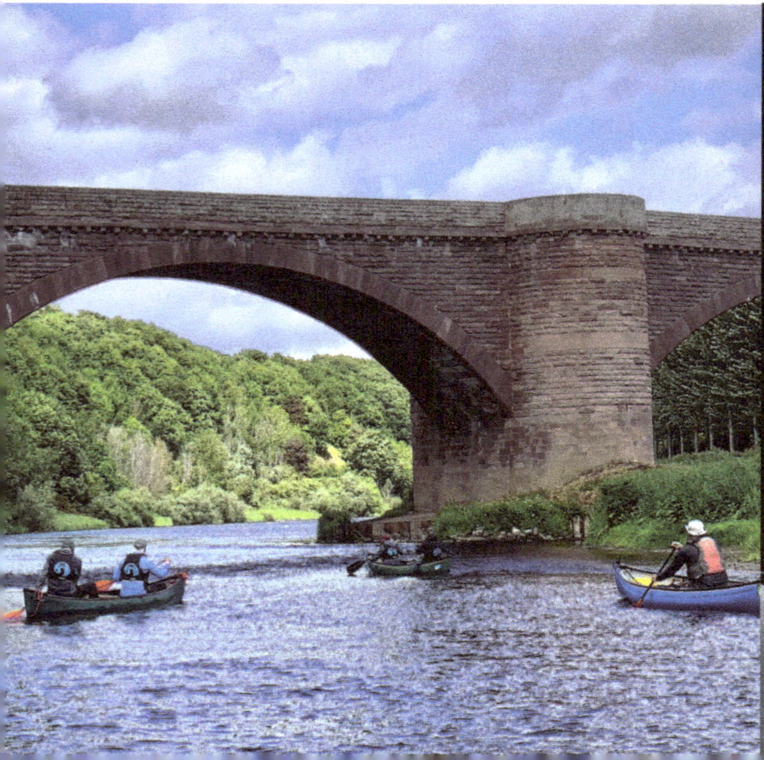
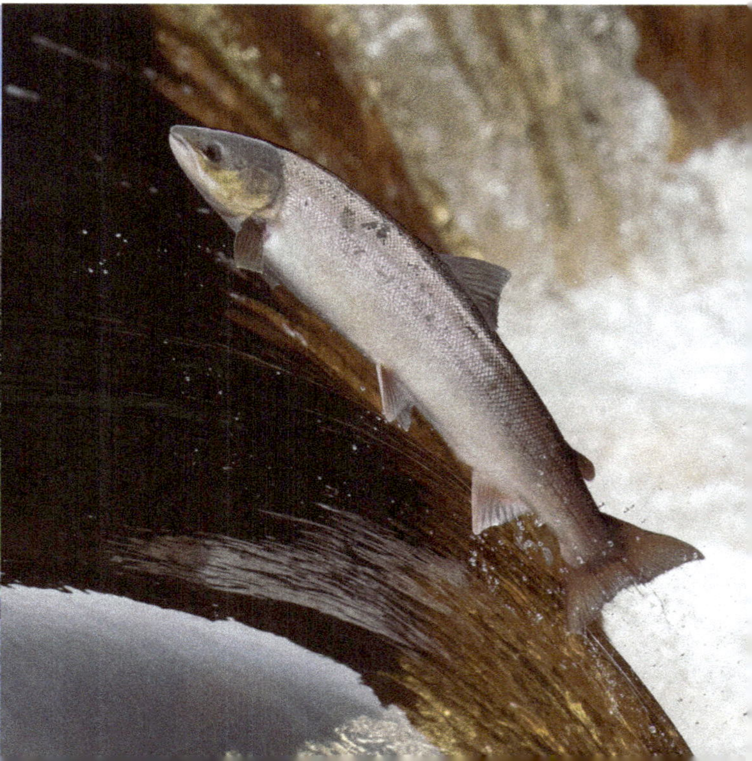

ACKNOWLEDGEMENTS

Simon Jarvis (Microlight Pilot) and Ollie Jay (Canoeist & Guide)

I wish to acknowledge the important part that both Simon and Ollie played in Tweed Trail Challenge. You will have already encountered Chapter 8 - Birdseye View and its counterpart Chapter 9 – An Otter's Perspective. Neither of which would have come about without the input, skill and expertise of these intrepid Gentlemen (Simon and Ollie). I am indebted to them for 2 truly wonderful experiences and highly recommend for others to embark on both adventures – magical.

Contact Simon via www.northumbriamicrolights.co.uk and Ollie via admin@active4seasons.co.uk

SPECIAL EDITION

THE
SABBATICAL

A Year of Travel During the Pandemic

James R. A. Herriot

PREVIOUS BOOKS BY THE AUTHOR
THE SABBATICAL
A YEAR OF TRAVEL DURING THE PANDEMIC

WWW.THESABBATICAL.CO.UK

INSIGHTS
TO KITCHEN DESIGN

SPECIAL EDITION

40+ Years in the World of a
Design-led Kitchen Specialist

James R.A. Herriot

PREVIOUS BOOKS BY THE AUTHOR
INSIGHTS TO KITCHEN DESIGN
40+ YEARS IN THE WORLD OF A DESIGN-LED KITCHEN SPECIALIST

WWW.INSIGHTSTOKITCHENDESIGN.CO.UK

For details of new and forthcoming books from Extremis Publishing, please visit our official website at:

www.extremispublishing.com

Follow us on social media at:

www.facebook.com/extremispublishing

www.linkedin.com/company/extremis-publishing-ltd-/

Subscribe to our regular newsletter at:

extremispublishing.substack.com

Hear our podcast on all good streaming audio providers

www.ingramcontent.com/pod-product-compliance
Lightning Source LLC
Chambersburg PA
CBHW061157010526
44119CB00059B/849